I AM
A GRACEFUL
BUTTERFLY

21 steps of healing to becoming free from your hurt, pain, trials, and tribulations; doing the soul work all while blossoming into a beautiful butterfly.

By:

Darshanelle Coleman-Boyer

ISBN: 9798734701928

Dedications

I would first like to thank my Lord and Savior Jesus Christ for birthing this book out of me and for entrusting me to deliver this book out to all of you. I would like to dedicate this book to my everything, my Great-Grandmother Ola Grace Cunningham, who is my angel in heaven. She was such a God-fearing, strong, powerful, giving, compassionate, kind-hearted grandmother and mother to many. My Great-Grandmother was a courageous, *tell it like it is*, woman. Thank you for taking me under your wing, instilling in me the tools I needed for life, and always being there when I needed you most. Thank you for seeing me, my gifts, my abilities, and my worth, even when I did not see it. Thank you for always praying constantly on your knees for me. Thank you for teaching me how to say my prayers at a young age and teaching me about God, making sure we went to church EVERY SUNDAY! You are the reason I am who I am today because of your love, support, and dedication. I love you so much, my Queen. I would like to also thank my Dad, Daryl Myron Johnson Jr., for raising me while still being a kid himself. Thank you for all you had to sacrifice, endure, live through, pray through, and fight through. Thank you for doing my hair when no one else was around to do it. Thank you for your constant love. Thank you for being patient with me when I was a teenager because you knew the challenges I was facing not having my mom in my life. Thank you so much. I will forever be indebted to you and Grandma Ola. The two of you are my earth angels.

I would like to acknowledge my wonderful loving husband, Steven Boyer, for being such an amazing God-fearing man, husband, father, son, and friend. Thank you for making sure I took the time I needed to bring this book to fruition and being my biggest cheerleader. Thank you for all you do, for it does not go unnoticed. You are my number one supporter, my best friend, my prayer partner, my business partner, my joy, my breath of fresh air, my everything. I love you, my king, with all of me. You make me such a happy woman to call you my husband. Thank you for loving me correctly and putting up with my imperfections and the best of me. I could not have asked for a more perfectly imperfect man for me. I am so grateful for the union and covenant we share under God.

I would like to dedicate this book to my mom, Lavarnia Coleman, for giving birth to me. I love you so much and thank you. I want to dedicate this book to my second mother, Dosshanda "TO-TO" Williams, for being there for me since I was a little girl up until now. Thank you for loving me as your own, for treating me with respect, honesty, loyalty and patience. I thank God for our connection because He knew we needed each other more than we could ever imagine. We have been in each other's lives through hard times and rewarding times. I am so grateful for you and I love you so much.

I would like to dedicate this book to my Aunt Tammy Malphurs, my Tam-Tam. Thanks so much for everything you have done for me. You have been such a big inspiration to my life, and you are my heart. I am thankful for our talks, the life lessons you taught me, and the business nuggets you have instilled in me. You know how I feel about you, and if no one ever tells you, I appreciate you; you know I always do. I love you so much!

To my Auntie Cornelia White, thank you so much for all the times you kept us in church, making sure we were fed the word at a young age, I did not get it then, but I get it now. You are my strength, my prayer partner, my talking buddy, and my sweet Auntie, who can do no wrong in my eyes. Your labor was not in vain. Auntie, you have been a great leader for our family. You passed the baton down, and I caught it, so thank you. I love you deeply, Auntie. Keep making God proud with that heart you have.

Acknowledgements

I would like to acknowledge and thank an incredibly special person near and dear to my heart. To my spiritual Mother, Terri Raven, and Pastor of "Terri Raven Ministries." I want to give a big thank you for all you have done, for being an inspiring, encouraging, real, transparent, loving woman of God. I admire the God in you, your obedience to God, and your dedication to serving us all in the way the lord would be proud of. Thank you for being such an extraordinary leader that shows what being a follower of Christ should look like. I just want to let you know that you have truly been a blessing in my life the past three and a half years. Thank you for praying for me, for covering me and my husband, and interceding on my behalf when I was going through so much in my life. Thank you for encouraging me to keep going and to not give up. I love and appreciate you so much more than what words can express. Terri Raven Ministries will always be near and dear to my heart.

To Mrs. Lisa Deans, thank you, thank you, thank you for everything you have done from your heart and sacrificed. Thank you for checking on me, praying with and for me, and for loving me as one of your daughters. You are such a beautiful spirit that I adore. Thank you for exemplifying the characteristics of Christ. I appreciate and love you.

I want to acknowledge Pastor Yvonne Scott-Miller of "One Lord Teaching Ministry." Thank you for pastoring me, being there for me and my family, for your prayers, and for all you sacrificed for me. I appreciate you dearly for being God's chosen vessel at the time in my life when I needed you and the God in you. Thank you so much. I love you.

I would also like to acknowledge and dedicate this book to all my siblings, my nephews and my niece. I love you all so much. To my sister/friend, Lattiea "Tiea" Whitaker. Thank you, Sissy, for your encouraging words, for being a shoulder to cry on, for always having my back, and for being there through it all. You are such a precious gem I did not know I needed. I love you and appreciate you so much. To my sister/friend, Antionette "Nia" Bing. Where do I begin? Thank you, sister, so much for being you and being there for me. Through the highs and the lows, you have been there. Through the tears and the smiles, you have been there. So, I thank you and love you so much. You have proved your loyalty, so for that, you will always have a special place in my heart. To my Rebecca "Becky" Peele. I love you so much you know you are my heart, and you will always have a special place in my heart. To my Grandma, all my aunts, cousins, supporters and family that I did not mention, you know I love you all deeply. I thank all of you so much for your prayers, love, and support. To my village, that is all of you, my graceful butterflies, that I have and have not met yet and those who are connected to me through the spirit. To those who will read this book, I love you and thank you so much. This is not my book. This is our book. We are in this together.

Intro

Hi, My Graceful Butterfly Queens,

I am Darshanelle Coleman-Boyer. I am 28, a wife, bonus mom, author, mentor, Certified Life Coach, business owner of The King and Queen Collection that I co-own with my husband. I am a believer, follower and ambassador for my Lord and Savior Jesus Christ, a prayer warrior, intercessor, encourager, motivator and leader. For some of you who read this book, I will be your sister. Some may adopt me as a daughter, a friend, your confidant, a listener, and even a midwife in the spirit to push you into greatness and becoming a better you. I would also like to say thank you for allowing me on this journey with you. I love you all and I want you to know I am your strength, and you all are the village I carry. This is our sacred place where you can be comfortable, transparent, real, raw and honest. This is a NO JUDGEMENT ZONE! A judgement-free space will be necessary to implement your new walk, while unpacking and trashing the things that can no longer serve those in your life. I too have gone through many challenges from a child all the way up to adulthood, from having four experiences where I could have lost my life in accidents but the Lord spared my life; from almost getting kidnapped or even getting raped when I was 18 by a guy friend at that time, but the lord covered me; from being raised without my mother and dealing with abandonment issues; to battling depression and anxiety for a long time. 2017 is when I hit rock bottom. This is when the enemy really played with my mind and had me in so much isolation and fear, telling me to commit suicide. He told me, "No one cares about you anyway." I would wake up in cold sweats, not being able to eat and afraid to go to sleep, and mostly every night, I would pray and cry myself to sleep. I felt misunderstood, overlooked, lied on, persecuted, attacked, and even talked about. I had to heal and forgive people that caused me pain. See, as I experienced all these challenges, people saw what I was going through and battling on the outside, but what they did not see was God doing a metamorphosis in me on the inside. I did not understand at that time because I was spiritually dead, but it was the anointing and mantle on my life that I knew nothing about. When the Lord sat me down and put this book in my spirit years ago, I was amazed at how He aligned my life with the stages that a butterfly goes through, and it blew my mind. I always say, "If I can transform into a vibrant, beautiful butterfly, anyone can." You have made a conscious decision to choose "YOU" in this process of "BECOMING." While on this self-love journey, you will learn to let go of the fears from your past that try to taint you. You will learn to become more confident in yourself and in God. You will learn to love yourself first at all cost. You will learn to become BOLD enough to walk in your excellence and own the queen you are that's deep within you. Most importantly, you will learn to see yourself from the same lens that our Father sees you. When you read this book daily for 21 days, without missing a day, you will find your true self that you could not even fathom, recognize or understand through being consistent. You will see that you have everything you need in you to produce much fruit to go ahead in faith. No, this road will not be easy. Daily, you will have to face yourself, re-visit scabbed or opened wounds that have been laying at bay, dig deep within yourself and be real all the way, forgive yourself and others, hold self-accountability for your actions, your healing and your future. You will let go of old, outdated habits and patterns and release the old you so you can spiritually grow and transform into the new you. This all sound so hard! I felt the same way while on my growth journey. It was challenging, but I must say, I am glad that I chose purpose rather than pain. I promise once you take the proper steps of healing correctly, it will become easier and easier with each day. Bet on yourself and give yourself 21 days if you're serious about doing something different to get better results out of life. You will feel great, act differently, and have a different walk. As a result, you will make healthy choices and decisions for your life and future that others will see as you transform. I am so proud of you for taking the first step to true healing, knowing there is a problem(s) that need to be addressed. I am so excited to see you have chosen "YOU" for a change, and for that, you will see an abundant outcome. Doing the soul work and looking at yourself in the mirror full of flaws, imperfections, scars, and wounds is the hardest but the most empowering, brave, and inspiring thing ever. Be proud of yourself because you have taken a step that many have not taken and probably will not take because of the pride they are holding on to or just not knowing how to take steps to get there. It all starts with you. ARE YOU READY? I HOPE SO! LET'S GO!

DARSHANELLE COLEMAN-BOYER

Table of Contents

The Preface

J ust as a Butterfly goes through four stages of life (Stage #1-
Egg, Stage #2 - Larva (caterpillar), Stage #3 - Pupa (chrysalis),
Stage #4 Adult) to become the beautiful butterflies we see flying
around during the Spring and Summer. We see them as the full-
grown butterflies with vibrant colors flying around without a care
in the world, but what we do not see is the process they had to go
through to get to the finished product of being the center of attention because of their eye-catching colors. No one ever talks about
the stressors butterflies may feel, the hurt they may endure, the im-
patience they must have to press through, the loneliness they may
encounter, or the unimportance they may feel while going through
the different stages. These factors are enough for us to be more
grateful and mindful of their growth process and not just see them
in their well-developed beauty stage. But to also see butterflies in
their not so pleasant stages when people don't care to see them or
even find them worthy.

As humans, I would say we share the same stages as a butterfly in our lives. We must go through a metamorphosis to get to that person that we know we can be and want to be. We, too, as humans, must go through the stressors of the world. We face challenges. We deal with hurts from our past, pain, unforgiveness, resentment, grudgeful ugly hearts and ways, brainwashed programmed minds, insecurities, fears, depression, anxiety, and so much more. While being faced with trials and tribulations, we do not often see the future potential we can grow into. We must keep the faith and not look at our current situation as the final result. We must know that we have the strength to overcome every obstacle and become that free-flowing, vibrant, beautiful butterfly that has no care in the world, and people will wonder and try to figure out who is this "NEW YOU." Did you know that butterflies go through a point in their stage where they are in hiding and not seen for a season because they are in their cocoon in a "RESTING STAGE?" While going through our transformation stage, there comes a time when people will not get to see or hear from you because God will have you set apart and hid so he can perfect you, prune you, and let your greatness from within shine when you have passed the test to your new level. The next time you are seen by the world, people will notice something is different, and you can tell them the secret - GOD AND SELF-LOVE IS THE BEST LOVE!

Allow this daily guide to help you adjust your crowns and become the queen you are. Let us do the Butterfly Effect together. YOU GOT THIS! Let's soar... II Corinthians 5:17

FUN BUTTERFLY FACTS:

In the egg stage of the butterfly's life cycle, a female butterfly lays her eggs, usually on stems of plants. Inside of the eggs are tiny caterpillars that grow and can vary in size, shape, and texture depending on the species. Some can be round, oval, cylindrical, smooth or bumpy. The time it takes the egg to hatch can also vary, and some only hatch when the weather gets warmer.

Stage 1

{THE WILDERNESS EXPERIENCE}

DISCLAIMER: This stage will be your hardest stage, but I promise it gets easier as you begin to confront those things that want to keep you bound. As I stated before, you will have to be real, honest, and very truthful in order to slay those demons and serve them an eviction notice to leave. When we go through a wilderness experience, we may witness financial, spiritual or emotional drought where nothing is going out, and nothing is coming in. It will seem as if everything you try to do is not working, nothing is happening, and you experience much loss. When you are going through this experience, nobody will be able to help you but God. It is a season where you feel alone in the natural and spiritual and God is perfecting you to lean only on him and not thinking for one second we can live life without him. I like to call this "THE AWAKENING" because your spirit will open on a spiritual level and God will begin to speak to you more and show you what he needs and want from you in the season you are in. When a person is walking through the wilderness, it simply means you have been tried by fire. You will go through many trials, tribulations and tests, all to prepare you for a season of greater, overflow, and success. The things you are experiencing are not to break you. They are only to get you to a place in God where he can get your attention and cause you to be obedient to him. Nothing you go through will be wasted. It is all for the greater glory of the Lord and to get you that place of elevation to the new version of you. The question is, how bad do you want it?

1.

Bring It All with You
(Withholding Nothing!)

All of us, at one time or another, have looked at our lives and wanted or needed a transformation to take place for us to become a new version of ourselves. Although these life changes may take time and be painful to endure, but when you can joyfully see how far you have come, in the end, you will be enormously proud of yourself.

You must learn to accept yourself and learn to be okay with every part of you that is imperfect and flawed but beautiful. Bring all your fears, baggage, insecurities, worries, resentfulness, hate, pride, arrogance, procrastination, jealousy, bad attitude, depressors, anxieties, your unfiltered words, doubt, your lack of confidence, and all the things that keep you trapped within yourself, dying to come out for freedom. When this takes place, you are stripped naked of all the things that tried to suffocate you and bury you with darkness. The first step to healing is acknowledging that there is an issue. This is the start of releasing all negativity and saying to yourself, "I do have issues and I know that by confessing with my mouth, I will prosper, and this will be the beginning of me becoming a beautiful butterfly." Running away to avoid your problems only makes more problems that build up to cause a bomb explosion within you. Do not run away from your problems because no matter where you go, no matter who you run to, or how far you go, your problems will still be there. So, the best thing to do is just accept them so you can move on and heal. See, the problem with the majority of society today is no one really wants to change and grow. People want a microwavable, right now version of healing and transformation, and no one wants to really face the ugly parts of them in exchange for the new and improved person they could become. There are people faking their healing and pretending they are okay when really, they are a wreck inside. How do I know? Because I was one of those people lying to myself when I really was dying on the inside needing help. I figured faking that I was healed was easier than facing myself and realizing, *girl, you are a hot mess*. I then realized I loved being free wholeheartedly and honestly versus the pressures of putting on a show and fooling nobody but myself.

Truth is, everyone is going through something, whether it's financial issues, grieving a loss, or being faced with mental health challenges. It may be big or small depending on each person's situation, but all are still valid. As you are going through this whole process, prayer is very much so essential because it can bring you over mountains and through valleys just to get you on the other side to see how beautiful life really is despite all the hell you had to go through to get there, all your hard labor will not be in vain. Your heavenly Father knows what is best for you, and he will see you through.

As you continue to walk with your shoulders up and your head held high, you will be on to the next step in completing your journey to true healing.

THE BUTTERFLY EFFECT:

Instead of trying to handle your problems on your own, try your heavenly Father, who is the ultimate problem solver! When we give our problems to him, we can go on in peace and faith, knowing that it is already done.

2.

Accountability is Key
(It's All on you)

As I have told you previously, we would have to take full responsibility for our own healing process and future. Accountability looks like taking ownership over your past trauma, abusers, pain, hurt, and heartbreaks even though it was not any of which you have caused. Holding ourselves accountable to regain power of our own lives is such a powerful position to be. I know that unimaginable things may have happened in your past and sometimes those things to overcome are extremely hard. We all have been victims of many things - rape, molestation, abandonment, motherlessness, Fatherlessness, addiction, low self-esteem, abuse and so much more. Everyone's pain will be different, but. You have me, and I know all about hurt and pain. I also wanted you all to see how far I have come with the help of God and those that constantly prayed for me and you can do the same thing. It is not by might or power but by the spirit of Jesus Christ that can free you, heal you and save you from all you are facing today if only you will let him in and believe.

Even though your past may have been traumatic, hurtful, and oppressive, it does not mean your future has to be buried under shame, lies, pain, depression, fear, doubt, low self-esteem and anxiety. Not addressing your pain properly can lead to a lack of coping skills that will later harm your life. This includes drugs, alcohol, poor life choices, and for some, following in the same cycles as your abusers. You must be the one where it ends and learn to face these things and have the willingness to overcome all obstacles in your life. Healthy coping skills vary from person to person, but for some, it may be seeking counseling, having a mentor or life coach, journaling, taking long walks, exercising, meditating, doing some inner soul searching, having an incredibly supportive social group you can trust. Whatever works best for you that is healthy and does not go against the will of God, I say go for it! You got this, and your past will not defeat you but rather help you push, press, and triumph over all your trials.

BUTTERFLY EFFECT:

You will never change your life until you change something you do daily. The secret to your healing is found in your daily routine.

FUN BUTTERFLY FACTS:

During the larva stage, which is the second stage of the butterfly cycle, the caterpillar leaves its egg home and enters the outside world. They literally eat their way out of the egg and start eating the leaves of the host plant. In this stage, they shed their skin four or five times. As the caterpillar grows, its skin becomes too tight and splits open revealing new, larger skin underneath. A fully grown caterpillar can be over 100 times larger than when it appeared from its egg.

Stage 2

{GROWING PAINS}

You have made it to the second stage in your healing process, and you should be jumping up and down proud of yourself for not giving up because I am sure the previous stage was a bit challenging. The growth stage is where you get to challenge yourself to be open and allow a new you to shine from within. As you continue on this road you will walk differently, talk differently, and have a whole new insight for your future. You will have more test, more trials, and more shortcomings in this stage, but the pressure is making you greater in God. The goal is to not give up. Step by step, with each step you take on this journey is taking you from glory to glory, elevating you to that place of purpose & destiny in your life. Let us move along to the next chapters where we dive a little deeper and go a little harder to tackle those things that are trying to keep you in constant cycles of being entangled. In this stage, it may feel like you are going through more pain than the previous stage, but it is a trick from the enemy to cause you to give up. Do not let him fool you. Pain is a sign that victory is just around the corner. You are closer to your breakthrough than you think, I declare and decree that you are free in Jesus name Amen.

3.

A Change of Heart

I will give you a little backstory of my testimony when I struggled with letting go of my grudgeful and resentful heart. When I
was around 14 or 15 years old is when I started to notice I had the
spirit of holding grudges and resentment towards my birth mother,
which later poured over to holding grudges towards people who
made me mad or upset. The feelings I had at that time very much
so had me burdened with unforgiveness, worry, hatred, denial,
loneliness, and just feeling abandoned and unloved. I had so many
questions and answers I had not received. All I wanted to know
was why I could not have my mother in my life like every other
girl I saw and resented. I do not think people really knew the pain I
went through not having a mother to be there to nurture me and
give me the love I needed and was searching for. I didn't get to go
on mother-daughter dates, have girl talks, and just overall have an
unbreakable bond. If your testimony is growing up without one or
both of your parents, you understand exactly just what I am saying.
It is one of those things you would have to go through to identify

with the magnitude of hurt you feel. So, around five years ago, I started my true inner healing. I had to face my issues of pain which had me intertwined in deep dark depression and anxiety that I had hidden within me to heal completely. I had to do the unimaginable, which was forgiving my mother fully for leaving me and not coming back for me, and that was one hard pill for me to swallow. It took a long road and lots of self-work to get to the healed place I am in with my mother. One day I just got to the point where I was tired of being tired, and I was fed up with myself. I was exhausted with being sad, mad, holding grudges, holding unforgiveness in my heart, and hiding how I truly felt, and I demanded change in my life, but it would first have to start with me. After I did this (one of the hardest things I had to do) I felt so much better because I did not allow anyone to have power over me. Instead, I let it go and let God do his thing.

In that time when I was going through my challenges, I had no one to talk to about my problems because I did not have an outlet where I really felt safe or no one to just listen to me without justifying the situation or telling me how to feel so I would keep everything bottled up inside pretending nothing was wrong. My dad raised me and did the best he could do, but he is a man and could not understand what I was dealing with from a young girl's perspective, so that was a void he could not fill. I tried filling it other ways, like talking to guys thinking they could give me the love I was so desperately needing, smoking weed, drinking, partying, and just being disobedient to the voice of God doing what I wanted to fill the void living in my own world. As I continued my growth journey, something stuck out to me that I never took into consideration. I was giving my mother grace despite what she did that I felt was not right because God had given me grace over and over many times while I was a hot mess. So, instead of giving my mother the short end of the stick, I extended my patience, forgiveness, my love, and my empathy to her. Sometimes we can be so deep in our own pain that we do not see others drowning in their own despair looking for a way out. We do not take-out time to hear someone else's story. I then begin to look deeper than myself and say to myself, "What happened to my mother when she was younger that she's not able to be a mother to her seven children?" Most times, how people turn out as adults stems back to things that happened to them as a child that they have not healed from. This is why it is important to heal so those things do not turn into generational cycles that will eventually be passed down to your children, your grandchildren, your village, those connected to you. One day while talking to my mom, I found out that she had a rough childhood. She had been molested by a family member and had gotten addicted to drugs and alcohol to numb all the pain she thought would go away, but made matters worse. She was suffocated by all the trauma that overtook her. When I found this out, I cried because I felt so bad for her. My heart hurts, knowing my mom had to endure much pain at a young age. It is something she is still battling and the pain is something we both shared. This was when I learned to love my mother more despite anything I felt that she fell short of or was not worthy of. I love my mom to life no matter what, and she will always have a special place in my heart. Self-healing is important at the instant we see something is wrong and is negatively affecting our lives. Most people do not heal because 99.9% of the time the pain is deemed too unbearable and facing ourselves and the things that happened to us is one the hardest things to do. What hurts me the most is that some people never find true healing. They live in denial, feeling unworthy, not feeling they are enough, and continuing to stay in cycles that keep them in the same circles, just in different seasons. We must eventually put the boxing gloves down, stare ourselves in the mirror, and speak to that younger girl inside of us that needs to be uncaged, loved, found, nurtured, seen and heard.

I know what you feel is valid because I know pain all too well. But instead of walking around with all that heaviness, you must release it, Sis. It is just not worth it! Life is too short, and you would regret not being able to speak to the person that hurt you if something tragic happened to them.. Free yourself and them while they are still here and alive because once they are gone, they are gone. If you are saying I cannot forgive my mother, my father or anyone who has hurt me, look within yourself and see how many times you messed up and God still forgave you and gave you grace (*II Corinthians 1:9*). If you do not know God or have a relationship with him, know that he is waiting on you to take the next step. He is calling for you, his beloved child. He loves you deeply. Try to look past you and dig deeper. Have a conversation with them to find out your parent's past and see what is blocking them from being a good parent to you. My prayer is that you will take my testimony and keep it with you so you can use it as inspiration to help you in your growth journey. Continue to be strong and courageous in everything, for everything we go through is not about us, but for those who need our stories to get through their trials, darkness, and hard battles, knowing they are not alone and will be blessed. You got this! Heal the right way, so you do not bleed on people that did not cut you.

THE BUTTERFLY EFFECT:

God is the only one who can turn our mess into a message
And our test into a testimony! Embrace your pain, your flaws,
And all you had to endure so that God can use it all for his glory!

4.

Attitude Be Gone

If I do not know anything else, I know all too well about this topic. Having an attitude and I were best friends, hunny! You couldn't tell me anything about it because I really did not care what anyone thought about it. My attitude was vicious. Now that I look back and think about it, I feel bad because I had an attitude with people that did not even deserve it. I let my negative emotions outpour onto others who were trying to help. I was going through my own baggage that I took it out on other people. Now that I am an adult and no longer in that place, I am quickly reminded when I am out at the store or wherever and I see people have a nasty attitude and spirit for no reason I look at them and start to get irritated, then quickly give grace and say, *wow that is how I use to be.* I had an ugly spirit and ugly attitude with a beautiful face and beautiful intentions, but the victim in me was bigger than the victor in me. At that time. My bad attitude was wreaking havoc in my life. It is so funny how life comes full circle and what you put out, you will get back. This applies to when you do good and when you do bad.

I said all of that to say, how you present yourself to the outside world is important because you never know who is watching you. Think about it, if people always seen you frowning, they will think you have an attitude whether you have one or not, and even probably assume you are rude, bitter or angry. Now, I know what some of you are probably thinking "I don't care about what other people think about me," and I somewhat agree. We should take note that this is not about what other people think at all, but most importantly about how you show up for yourself in the world. Do not let what you've been-through control your future because it is just not worth it, Queens! How we show up in the world depends on us. What we draw into our day/life depends on us and the energy we are put out. What people we come across, whether we are welcoming blessings in our life or pushing them away, is all on us, and the list continues. So, we must make sure we are doing our part and being the change we want to see in the world.

Can you promise me something? Okay, I am glad you said yes! If I told you that your attitude will either bring you blessings or roadblocks, would you change it? Great job! I am thrilled you made the right decision. There is so much happiness in life from this end of the rainbow, and as you start to have a more positive, vibrant, fun attitude towards life, it will treat you great. Let us keep it real, having a negative and nasty attitude will only cause people not to want to be around you and not like you. You will most likely spend a lot of time alone as I did. I am so happy that you are doing something new to get better results for your life.

P.S. Changing your attitude does not make you immune from life's trials and tribulations. It helps us look at life from a different set of lenses to better handle the tests we face.

When we free ourselves from all the bondage and captivity, we then will start to see that having a great attitude makes you feel good and look good. When we present ourselves to the world in a light where we have a smile on our face and our spirits are lifted like a ray of sunshine, it makes socializing with others easier, it makes people addressing you easier, it makes communication easier, and it makes life easier.

Wearing your smile is such a powerful accessory, so never leave home without it. Jumpstart your day every day with a smile because you never know when someone may need your smile for motivation, encouragement, or to feel cared for or loved. You just never know. I know we all have dealt with some level of pain, agony, heartbreak, or hurt, but we must push beyond the surface and fight to be greater. Do not let the pain from your past be the answer to your future. You are not a victim, but you are victorious in the Lord (*Romans 8:37*).

THE BUTTERFLY EFFECT:

It takes 43 muscles to frown and 17 to smile. Which one will you choose today?

5.

Unlearn to Relearn
(Breaking Generational Cycles)

In this chapter, we will talk about breaking generational cycles and curses off your life. See, we do not get the luxury of choosing the family we are born into, but luckily as we get older, we can choose to trash things we have negatively adopted that no longer suits us and keep the things that were ordained over since we were in our mother's womb and make us who we are. A generational cycle is something that negatively affects a family that passes down from generation to generation, and a lot of times, it is a tough stronghold to break until someone stands up and says enough is enough! The cycle stops with me. Some examples of negatively generational cycles are getting pregnant at a young age, generational cycles of poverty, alcohol and drug addiction, absentee parents, division in families, middle and high school dropouts, generational cycles of verbal, financial lack, mental, and spiritual or physical abuse in families to name a few.

You can look at the list above and attest that those things are true. Two or three may even stand out to you because you notice these negative cycles tugging at your family. You know the same way there can be a negative impact on the generations in your family, there can be positive ones as well. You can create generational wealth and a legacy that breaks the cycle of lack and poverty. You can break the spirit of addiction over your life, your children's life and those lives who are attached to you. You can make different choices and decisions to have better results in your life, but you must first be willing to be different and beat the odds of doing away with old patterns that lead to old roads. You may look at yourself and say, "I have some generational cycles that I need to break." You can do it because you are victorious, and you have the power within you to do so. If you really want to change and break those cycles, ask God to help you because he is the only one who can. You must have prayer, patience, diligence, power, speak with authority, perseverance, consistency, and the willingness to want change. It is not an easy task, but it can be done if you are serious about wanting these cycles gone from out your life.

I want to share a little of my testimony of me having to break generational cycles off my life and my bloodline. My mom was 15 years old when she got pregnant with me, and my dad was 16 years old. Both came from an absent parent home that left them repeating some cycles they did not even realize was eating away at their lives and children's lives. See, my mom came from a background where she grew up without her dad and where her mom battled with drug and alcohol addiction. So, my mom repeated those cycles of addiction. The streets raised her at a young age. My dad, on the other hand, grew up being fatherless and not having his mom there like he wanted. He was raised by my great-grandma Ola, leaving him to grow up faster than he was supposed to. He also became a teen parent. My dad unknowingly was following in the footsteps of his dad because, at a young age, he became addicted to alcohol to suppress the pain he was fighting inside unknowingly from all the childhood trauma he faced. Both of my parents are amazing souls who just had a hard upbringing that some can overcome, and others do not because the pain is too hard to face. The ending to your story does not have to be a bad one. Rather the whole trajectory of your story can be changed when you hold yourself accountable, shift your mindset, and not settle for anything less than what you are supposed to have or be in this life.

After reading a little of my mom and dad's testimony, I know, just like other people, you probably thought I would be a product of a generational cycle, but I would like to say I am where the cycle ended. Even though I went through many trials, tribulations, tests, imperfections, flaws, and moments where I was a hot mess, I was always determined to be better than my parents and the environment where I grew up, and I say that humbly. I always told myself I'm going to graduate high school (I did in 2011). I told myself I did not want to be a teen mother and that I didn't want to have kids until I was married (I got married February 14, 2020 and my husband and I will have kids at God's desired time). I told myself I wanted to go after my dreams and purpose. I am doing just that (I started my first business in May 2020 called The King & Queen Collection and I became a Certified Life Coach in April 2020). I am a mentor to young girls and women under my Grace 4 You Hotline & Outreach Center Corporation. I became an author in 2021. I have a youth life coaching business that I started in 2021. I have a prayer line where we meet for prayer every Monday at 7 am, and I am walking in my purpose in ministry, working for the kingdom spreading God's word. I am not boasting, but I'm bragging on Jesus because he did it, and it was nothing but the grace of God. I want to encourage you to not give up on yourself or your dreams because God will help you achieve them all. You don't have to be a product of your environment. I came straight from the "HOOD" in Norfolk, Virginia, called Roberts Park Projects. Many people don't make it out. Most let their dreams die and never go after them, but I have always been determined and wanted more than the cards I was being dealt. I always knew there was more for me and to me, and I am grateful because my childhood taught me so much. It showed me how to persevere, be determined, be grateful, be humble, and how to be a fighter and champion. You can choose if you want better or make an excuse as to why you must be accustomed to repeating a cycle that was meant to end with you. Just because you want better does not mean you think you are better than anyone. It means you see more; you see the light and you see better in yourself. God thinks you are better. That is why he is challenging you now to put down the boxing gloves and surrender to his call over your life. You are different, unique, favored, set apart, and peculiar for a reason. This is why the attack on your life has been so strong since you were a child. The enemy may be fighting you with depression, anxiety, fear, loneliness, doubt, and all kinds of insecurities, but I declare and decree that the power of God is going to hit your life suddenly. You have not seen your best days yet. Every word curse that was spoken over your life, I denounce it powerless in the realm of the spirit, and I return to sender 100-fold in Jesus name, Amen. When I say the enemy cannot do anything with you because you are a child of God, I mean just that. WALK IN YOUR POWER, QUEEN!! YOU GOT THIS!

This is your new season to walk in your anointing, your power, success, wealth, healing, miracles, overflow, and to walk in your season of prosperity. Fight and push your way through. Hang on to every ounce of faith you have without letting go. You are birthing something new and you cannot abort your baby in the spirit in this season. Someone needs what you have inside of you to keep going. Someone's breakthrough is in your testimony. You are too close to give up now. I am here with you, Queen. Hold on and be strong. I am standing in the gap with you. It all stops with you, so embrace your new life.

THE BUTTERFLY EFFECT:

When they say it runs in the family, you tell them, "This is where it runs out." Don't let others label you when you have been identified by God.

6.

Process of Elimination
(Just throw it in the trash)

As children, when we grow up, we were often brainwashed in our homes, in our society, in the government, religious systems, schools, and more. Our minds were programmed with channels we could not even get the correct signal to. These things lead us into adulthood, causing us to act in ways that are not beneficial for our future. It may also have caused us to make bad choices in our adolescent, teenage and adult lives. Do you agree that some things our parents, grandparents, and family members have taught us and shown us were not the best advice to give us? When I got older and started my own growth and healing journey, I noticed and took inventory of all the things in my life, putting the must-haves on one side and the garbage that needed to be trashed on the other side. It was hard giving up those things I have kept as a keep-sake for so long because that is how and what I was raised on. These false imprisonments caused our minds to be clouded with gray skies that have no trace of sunshine. Just throw it in the trash, the lies, old religious traditions, everything that has been causing you to think, act and speak wrongly.

When I was growing up, my great-grandmother was who I saw make it all happen and who I called superwoman. Back then, she was very independent. She had a big heart and would do anything for anyone. She was soft but stern. I never saw her soft side. I never saw her be weak or submit to any of her male friends. She always told us, "You do not need a man for anything and that you go get your own." Grandma did not mean any harm. She was only teaching us what she was taught, and I believe she wanted to keep us from getting hurt as well. See, this right here is why I did not have relationships long because I used to tell guys, "I don't need a man; I can make it happen on my own!" That was my attitude. I became aggressive, controlling and things had to go my way or the highway in relationships. While doing some self-reflection, I had to sit back and say to myself, *this is not the right way at all*. One of the best things about being an adult is getting to make the right choices, even if that means getting rid of the old ones. I let my pride down and became gentler, less aggressive, and let my humility take its course in my life. Truth is, a woman needs a man, and a man needs a woman because God created us to need one another. Saying we do not need a man is a defense mechanism women use to keep ourselves from getting hurt, but when we allow God to bring our BOAZ and not search for him on our own, a true match is made in heaven (*Genesis 2:18*).

One other major eliminator I had to get rid of was the "What goes in this house stays in this house" mentality. Now, this one ruined me because it taught me how to deal with things internally, not knowing how to communicate or express how I felt. This was one of the reasons I battled depression and anxiety that was silently trying to defeat me. I did not want anyone to know what I was dealing with it. I feared judgement and the "she's crazy" stigma. I went to speak to a counselor, my pastor at the time, and a few people I know. This helped me to be able to express my feelings in a better way. I learned how to not run away from my truth or the things I was going through because it makes the problems worst. When we learn how to face the depression, anxiety, and all the things that try to keep us bound, we learn that the circumstances become more attainable. It helps us find a better solution to our problems - and that is Jesus. Fighting battles in silence is torture, and it sometimes feels like a punishment because that is the enemy's way of making us feel like we have no one or no one will care if we speak about it, but we do not have to because our heavenly father gave us options. You can always find someone we trust, a counselor, a friend, or a life coach who can help you because you do not have to suffer in silence. If you or someone you know are fighting a battle that no one knows about, I would like to encourage you. I want you to know that as much as it seems that you are alone, you are not! God is there and he hears your cries and silent battles you fight. Give all your worries and cares to him so he can see you through. Everything you are going through is for a purpose. You are supposed to be here because someone needs the greatness that is inside of you, and someone needs your strength to go on. Someone needs that story that is inside of you. So, keep pushing and do not give up, Queens (*1 Peter 5:7*).

Let's go an elimination diet, shall we? This is where you will eliminate things from your life that no longer serve your purpose. Sometimes those things are people, old mindsets, old attitudes, outdated programs, guilt, shame, worry, resentment, blame, regret, and the list continues. I know from experience that God can also use our weaknesses and flaws to make us more beautiful while giving us beauty for ashes (*Isaiah 61:3*) when we embrace our weaknesses and allow him to do a work in us and through us. The great thing about eliminating something is that we have room that allows God to add to our lives as he refines and perfects us. Be transformed by the renewing of your mind, as it states in *Romans 12:12*. Renewing our mind is simply shifting and elevating it from a place of stinking thinking, overthinking, negative thinking and replacing it with positive words, affirmations, and only meditating on things that are pure, right, admirable, lovely, noble and true enter into your mind, body, and spirit (*Philippians 4:8*). In life, we must take the good with the bad and use our inadequacies to bring about a whole new meaning in our lives. See, I know it is easier to blame our parents, grandparents, and family members for their case of knowingly or unknowingly brainwashing us, but they were just teaching us what was taught to them. It is our jobs as young adults and women to take our power back and stand up for what is right, even if that means standing alone and beating the odds in your family and community. Will you be brave? Are you that one? I believe in you, Sis! You've got my support because that is what sisters do - support one another.

THE BUTTERFLY EFFECT:

The hardest part is always letting go, but once you do true beauty and freedom await you on the other side.

7.

Forgiveness

What is forgiveness?

Forgiveness is an intentional, conscious, and voluntary decision to release feelings of resentment, hate, anger, or vengeance towards a person or group of people who have harmed you, whether they deserve your forgiveness or not. Forgiveness does not mean pretending everything is okay, and it does not mean forgetting the hurt either. Forgiveness is simply the act of surrendering our desire for revenge; that is our desire to hurt someone for hurting us. Forgiving others is the gift we give to ourselves that enables us to stop picking at the scab and arrange a plan for true self-healing. When we forgive, it is not for the other person. It is for us and allowing ourselves to be free in our mind, heart, body, and spirit.

In the Bible, God talks about how we are forgiven for our sins. God also said, "If we want to be forgiven, we must first forgive others (*Matthew 6:14-15*). One thing for sure and two things for certain, we cannot argue with God or his word because "HE SAID WHAT HE SAID!" And that settles it. The proof is in the pudding, which is the Holy Bible!

Let's keep it all the way real, Queens, we all have wanted revenge one time or another on the people that have hurt us. I can attest and say at a time in my life before my growth journey, I would want that because I would want them to hurt how I was hurting. To be clear, I never wanted anything harmful to happen to anyone. I just wanted them to feel a little something for what they did, but who am I? I have fallen short of the glory of God all the time. I do not think I am alone in feeling this way either. I know many of you have felt that way in the past, or you may be feeling that at this very moment. I must say to you that this way of living is just not healthy at all because it does nothing positive for you or your spirit. If you want to know if you have truly forgiven someone, try out this test below.

When you forgive:

You know you are free from unforgiveness is when the person(s) is around you, they will not change your spirit, attitude, or body language. You will walk in pure joy, happiness, freedom, light, and you will be able to treat them with kindness, humility, and respect.

When you do not forgive:

When you have not forgiven your offenders, their presence will shift your spirit, attitude, or body language to a whole other level. You can be in a happy space, and as soon as you see their face, it will make you mad, sad, angry, and livid. You will relive the past hurt they have caused you.

Between the two, which one are you? Have you truly forgiven, or do you need work in this area? What is stopping you, Queen? It is all on you! Choose the one that will excel you and propel your future.

Now I know all of you who are holding on to unforgiveness is looking at me side-eyed, with the stink face, saying, "WHAT? DO YOU KNOW WHAT THEY DID TO ME?" Hunny, I know that look and that frustration. TRUST ME! This is all for the betterment of your life, and you will look back and be glad one day that you chose forgiveness over negative emotions towards someone. Forgiveness is one of the hardest things I ever had to do, and that is on the real note. I figured if I could forgive my mother, I was capable of forgiving anyone. When I was walking around mad at everyone carrying around all those negative emotions, it felt like I had 1,000 pounds of bricks weighing on my shoulders. Did you know caring around anger, bitterness, hate, and unforgiveness is one of the causes of sickness that people carry in their bodies and minds? While you are sitting at home mad, sad, crying, and going through the motions, you know what they are doing? They are out, living without a care in the world; living carefree while you are still in this place of unforgiveness. Do yourself a favor and do not allow anyone to have power over you, but instead take charge over your life and every situation. If you need help with forgiveness, take it to the Lord in prayer and I promise he will show you the way.

Some people say it is too hard to forgive, but I would like to say it is too hard not to. Let go and let God!

THE BUTTERFLY EFFECT:

When you forgive, you empty yourself so that you
can receive all that has been destined for you.

FUN BUTTERFLY FACT:

In the third stage of the butterfly cycle, once fully grown, the caterpillar forms itself into a "pupa" or "chrysalis," a kind of vessel in which the caterpillar changes into a butterfly. They usually do this on twigs or safe hidden areas around the host plant. The pupa stage may last for a few weeks or several months, depending on the species. During this time, a hardened case forms around the pupa to protect it from predators and harsh weather conditions. Inside, the tissue, limbs and organs of the caterpillar transform into a beautiful, winged butterfly.

Stage 3

{TRANSITION & BIRTHING}

Hey Queen, you feel alright? That is great! You are almost to the end. You should give yourself a big pat on the back for choosing to keep pushing past the pain, the hurt, the anger, the lies, setbacks, and roadblocks. As your sister, I want you to know that I am rooting for you with my pom-poms in my hands on the frontline. Now, in this stage of transition and birthing, you will have to push harder, fight in the spirit, pray a little longer, and have much faith. As you are transitioning, you will start to see and notice that you are feeling more of God. You are seeing him more and experiencing him in a new way. You will also start to see everyone you thought was for you is not. Your appetite and spirit will not have the same taste for things and people as it once did. You will see that some people will not be happy for your growth because it is easier for them to keep you at that past level you once were. God is doing something new and amazing in your life, and I do not care if no one support you or cheer you on, know that I am here for you and I mean it. This stage is also going to teach you a lot about yourself because you have so many gifts, talents and abilities locked inside of you that are lying dormant. In the end you will see why you had to endure so much to get to this place you are right now, because it will all come full circle. Follow me into the next chapter where things get a little bumpy yet beautiful.

8.

Healing Anyone?

While on this journey and in life, you are responsible for your own healing. Despite what others have said or done, you have to take control of your healing because It will not be handed to you. If you do not take control, who else will? Below I have listed eight steps that will help you jumpstart the process to freedom, and that is total healing. When you learn to Acknowledge, Desire, Accept Responsibility, Pray, Identify, Forgive, Resolve, and have gratitude, you have the keys that will unlock all those mental, spiritual, physical, and emotional roadblocks. C'mon, let's dive a little deeper, shall we?

Acknowledge: The first step to healing is being aware that there are problems and issues that need to be addressed. At some point, you must look at your life and see there is a problem with the merry-go-round cycles in your life. For instance, when an alcoholic goes to an AA meeting or an addict goes to a NA meeting, the first thing the instructor is going to tell them to do is to acknowledge that they have a problem so they can continue on to the next steps of healing. This is the most powerful step because it allows you to yield and no longer be able to run and hide. This step cannot be overlooked. You must face this first step to complete any other step.

Determination & Desire: Secondly, you must aspire and truly desire to want the healing, or you will not get the proper healing that you are supposed to have. You will also not have the correct amount of motivation for healing if the desire is not there. For instance, when I reached out to this program to get my mom help, the lady first said to me, "Does she want to change?" I pondered that question because I knew as much as I wanted her to change, she had to want it as much as I did.

Accept Accountability: There must come a point and time when we stop blaming others and situations and take responsibility for our actions, decisions, and beliefs. We must stop looking at that outwardly mere image and start looking inwardly at ourselves. Playing the victim will not be our forte anymore. We are walking victoriously and mighty in our true, wholesome selves we were called and created to be.

Pinpoint: Identify the areas where you need true healing. I mean, get real raw and honest with yourself. You know you better than anyone and being real is the only way this healing process is going to work. Do you feel unworthy? Do you have anger issues? Do you feel insecure? Do you have low self-esteem? What are those areas you can reflect on and get help in?

Forgive: Forgiveness is important, and it is imperative that you forgive yourself and others.

Pray: All your efforts, progress, and accomplishments will be magnified if you would include your heavenly Father, who is always working on your behalf. If you pray and ask for his guidance and assistance, he will always be there without a shadow of a doubt. He is such a good loving Father, and you are so special to him. He is always right near you, and trust and believe, he will never leave nor forsake you (*Deuteronomy 31:6*).

Resolve: Coming up with a resolution plan to resolve any issues you have lingering around is important. Get to work and finish strong, and if you must revert to any of the techniques from above, do that also.

Gratitude: When we find ourselves with an attitude of gratitude, we position ourselves to receive greater. We must express gratitude in every little step, experience, circumstance, test and trial, for they all become our teachers, for life is a learning journey. Do you have a grateful heart on today?

After reading the steps of healing above, do you think you can be fully committed to those things to activate your healing process so you can feel better about yourself for a change and not hide the real you inside? Which is the hardest part for you in the steps? Will you stay consistent? I believe in you wholeheartedly that you can do it. Doing these steps properly will also help you with showing up in the world with a heart of gratitude, compassion, integrity and empathy.

THE BUTTERFLY EFFECT:

Healing does not mean the damage never existed.
It means the damage no longer controls our lives.

9.

Self-Love is the Cure

After healing properly from the inside, you will be able to provide self-care to yourself and love on "YOU" more. I think we are all guilty of emptying our cups to fill others up even when we have nothing much to offer ourselves. Then, the question remains, "Who is going to fill me up?" As women, we are natural nurturers, and we tend to enable those around us without notice most of the time. We have been taught many things in our childhood, but one thing most of us have not been taught was how to love ourselves properly. I am not talking about dressing up our outer being with clothes, make-up, fly shoes, a nice bag, and accessories like I did. I am simply talking about loving us wholeheartedly from the inside from the depths of our soul. Being okay with not being the prettiest girl in the room, having the smartest intellect, not having the longest hair, or not having the nicest body shape. When you love yourself, flaws and all, this love cannot be replaced. When you love how God created you, you do not have to change your physical being to accommodate anyone or to fit into a world where society is not normalizing true beauty from within. I want to share a quick story with you. When I was in my early teenage years, around 10-17 years old, I dealt with low self-esteem. I did not think I was worthy. I did not like my skin complexion at all because with the world we live in today wants to separate us and prefers lighter skin over darker skin complexions. This is something most young girls and woman who are more on the brown or darker skin tone have endured. Many feel insecure about their dark skin. When I think about it now as an adult, it stemmed from first not having my mother in my life or no one at a younger age to instill in me that I was beautiful. So, I went searching for a boy to tell me I was beautiful because I did not get that at home. My dad told me sometimes, but not often, so it was not believable to me when he said it. I felt like he was my dad, so he had to tell me that. My low self-esteem was also because I use to get teased by some of my cousins that would call me black and fat because I was a little chunky when I was younger. Even though I pretended like it did not hurt, deep down, it crushed me, made me sad, and sometimes I would cry to myself. One day, when I was talking to my Aunt Becky, who has lighter skin, I told her I did not feel pretty. She looked at me and said, "You are beautiful, Darsh. You look like me!" People would say we favored a lot by some of our features. She would always tell me how beautiful I was. The part I respect about her the most is even though she did not know how I felt because she has lighter skin, she embraced me and made me feel beautiful in that moment. I am so grateful that I had her in my life at that time because I now know my true beauty through God, and the skin I am in is so gorgeous. I am a masterpiece. Can I tell you something today? Do you know you are beautiful just the way you are, your skin completion and the way it glistens against the sun, your eyes whether they are big, small, bright, or dark they are beautiful, your smile that light up any room you walk in, your hair whether its kinky, coily, straight, curly, long or short you are still beautiful so rock your beauty, you are intelligent, smart, fearless, brave, powerful, anointed and a prized masterpiece? We are normalizing true beauty, which is self-love, and if you follow me deeper into the chapter, I am going to give you some examples of things you can do to love on yourself.

There is no greater love than when you love yourself. Whether other people love you or not, self-love is the greatest love of all. When you view yourself as a Queen, a creation, a piece of art, a sculpture, you will know how to value yourself and set morals. Being you is what makes you unique, and when you try to adapt to the outside world of people, you become trapped into the norm. It is okay to be different, it is okay to be who you were created to be, and it's okay to be an unapologetically beautiful person inside and out. I do not care what social media has said, but beauty comes in all shades of colors and different sizes, so be confident in your beauty!

Having respect for yourself will carry you a long way in life, but you have to love yourself, or nobody will. Self-love and beauty are more than your thighs, hips, and how cute your outer appearance may look. Those things are just part of the genetic makeup of who you are but does not define who you are. Your morals, values, standards, characteristics, personality, and beliefs make you who you are inwardly. Let me ask you a question, if you do not love yourself, how can you love somebody else? A lack of self-love in one's life is low self-esteem. You de-value yourself and demoralize yourself. You accept things that are not sufficient for you or your future. Sis, I am telling you this from experience, do not settle for things that God will not be pleased with, for things that will cause you more pain than joy. Sometimes, we must practice being with ourselves and loving ourselves to the point we do not care who walks away if we know God is there. What I have learned on this journey is all company is not good company, and we must be extremely careful about who we let in our space, time and energy. Some people only want to plug into your energy source to drain you and use you of the power and destiny that is within you. Release anyone from your life who is draining your energy physically, mentally and spiritually. Those people are a liability (you are losing with them being added to your life) and not an asset (you are gaining with them being in your life).

Outside of the love that our heavenly father has for us, self-love is the best love we will ever experience. I know trying to love yourself may be hard because you may not have been taught these gems because mama was not there to be the example, daddy was not there to show you what real love from a man was supposed to feel like. Perhaps your innocence was taken from you by a tragic situation in your life, or you may know what love is but have lost yourself along the way. Whatever your story is, know that it is not too late, and this is the time to go after the love you need and have been looking for all this time, and is loving you. You are no good to anyone if you do not love you and take care of yourself. In *Mark 12:31* it says, "Love your neighbor as yourself." This will depend on how much we love ourselves. We can only love our neighbor with the measure of love we know, and most of the time, it is not a lot because it is love from the world's view with conditions. It was not from God's view, which is unconditional. No matter what your situation or circumstance is, you are an overcomer of any stumbling block that may try to make you feel inadequate. Do not let what those people did to you cause you to lack love within yourself. Do you know how needed you are in the world? Do you know you are so special and loved? You are a queen, a royal priesthood that is fearfully and wonderfully made. Do you know your heavenly Father loves you so much and care for you? When you are down, he is down. When you are happy, he is happy, and when you are rejoicing, he is also rejoicing with you. You are not alone and know that "This too shall pass."

Oftentimes, we tend to look for love in all the wrong places to try and fill a void that is never filled until we get the true healing we need. I remember turning 18 years old, graduating high school, and going through some personal issues trying to find my identity, trying to find my mother in the streets of Norfolk, VA, and looking for love in the wrong places when all that was a temporary fix. At that time, being young, I thought guys telling me all the things that were fleshly like you're pretty, you have a nice shape, you dress nice, you should come chill at my house, do you smoke, or drink and all the other game they tried to pull when they want something was flattering. All these lusts filled emotions were the attention I thought I needed to fill that emptiness of not feeling loved properly by my mom or dad or anyone at the time. I was looking for someone to say "I love you" or looking for someone to validate the greatness inside of me. I was suffocating in my own despair, that I was falling for things a guy told me that I knew was not right, but I let loneliness make a fool of me. Do not let unhealed wounds cost you your life and have you forgetting about your self-worth and respect. Please do not fall for the trap; it is an illusion. I am telling you this because I do not want any of you to go through the same mistakes as I did. It is the curiosity, disobedience, rebellion, and disrespect that get you entangled in webs you cannot find an exit to. The moral of the story is your validation and approval are only needed for God to see and not man because man will lie to you. God always keeps his Word. If he said he is going to do it, trust and believe he is going to do it. Trust and believe him at his Word.

Do you know some exercises you can practice exemplifying self-love towards yourself? The first step for me was looking at myself and telling myself. I LOVE YOU. I AM WORTHY. I AM ENOUGH. I AM BEAUTIFUL. I AM NEEDED. I AM POWER-FUL. Saying these things really set the foundation for me for where I was in my life at that time. This was before my spiritual walk, so I was not aware of my identity in God and who I was in him. It was when I found who I was in him that made those powerful words I said to myself stand out and have meaning and spirit behind them. When doing this exercise, it shifts your mind from self-love abuse to becoming whole, happy, and healed from the depths from within.

The second step to self-love for me was having the highest level of self-respect for myself. Self-respect for me was being intentional about how I showed up in the world with the way I dress and the way I act, respond and communicate with others. Respecting yourself is taking pride in keeping your body and temple healthy. Making sure that our minds, bodies, and spirits are all aligned and flowing in the right direction. Also, being responsible enough with our bodies and saving ourselves from the different spirits we let enter our temples and waiting until marriage to journey down that road of holy matrimony and covenant unto God. I remember saying to myself one day, "I wish I would have waited for sex until I was married!" I lost my virginity when I was 19 years old, out in the world living in my flesh, knowing what I was doing was wrong and knowing that God said in his word to not have sex before marriage (1 Corinthians 6:18-20, 1 Corinthians 7:8-9). Do you know sex is a gift from God? Sex was designed to be between a married woman and a married man to be under a covenant that honors and follows God. Do not let anyone fool you and tell you that having sex is bad. It is only bad when it is done outside the will of God and doing it not being married or if you are married and committing adultery. When we are in the single season of our life, we are supposed to have self-control and remain celibate until God sends us our spouse, whom he has designed for us. Another indication that marriage and family are a gift; a beautiful thing because God said that he wants us to be fruitful and multiply (Genesis 35:11). What some do not understand is sex is a spiritual transfer between a man and a woman, and when you lay down with someone who is not your spouse, you transfer your spirit to them, and they transfer their spirit to you with negative unwanted soul ties. When I was faced with some health issues 4 or 5 years ago, I was led to be celibate until God sent my husband to me, and five years later, with mistakes, highs and lows, I am married to the love of my life because of God's love, grace, and promise over my life. The best thing I could have done was wait on God to send my husband because, in the past, I have made a mess of things trying to find my spouse myself. When I was willing to give up everything to focus on my relationship with God is when he did the unthinkable in my life because I let nothing stand in the way of that anymore. I allowed myself to be in a place that was uncomfortable and unfamiliar to be positioned for a blessing and a gift of marriage. If God allowed me to go through that test and rewarded me know that he is no respecter of persons and will do the same for you if you trust, sacrifice, and believe. He wants to use you as an example that it can be done, but the question is: will you let him?

Lastly, I would say this one is like the icing on the cake because it put you in a position of doing things for yourself whether you are a mom, whether you are single with no kids, whether you are married, old, young, man or woman. Self-care is the most important part of loving yourself because if we do not take care of ourselves, neither will anyone else. I remember a couple of years back before I ever knew about self-care because I was not taught. I thought I would look weird taking myself on a date but let me say they were some of the best times I spent with myself. It allowed me time to step away from loving on everyone else and love on myself, it gave me the time and ability to be able to feel and take in all that was going on in me and around me, it allowed time for me to talk to God and thank him and love on him more, I could go on and on, but I just wanted to let you in on my perception of being alone and in love with me. Do not let anyone make you feel bad for taking time out with "YOU" when I say no one, I mean just that. Not your spouse, your children, your job, your parents, your siblings, your friends, NO ONE! Think about it, before you had all these roles and responsibilities, it was just you and God (whether you knew it or not, he has always been there with you, guiding, protecting, and shielding you. He never leaves us, we leave him) let me ask you a question I want you to take some time to think about: what is stopping you from taking time out to love on yourself today? Why do you feel guilty? Do you feel like you are not worthy of self-care? Whatever the case may be, I want to let you know that even a dog gets tired. I can feel prophetically that many of you are tired, exhausted, burnt out, codependent, and do not know how to take time out with yourself, pouring from an empty cup, and crying loud but no one can hear or see you slowly drowning. I want you to know I feel your pain because I was once there, and now is the time for you to rise up in your power, focus on you for a change. Know that you have the right to love yourself first before anything or anyone. You cannot keep pouring from an empty cup because your well will eventually run dry. Deposit some time, love, joy, and happiness into yourself. The only way to do this is to find ways to do things with yourself, so you can allow God to speak to you, fill you back up, and show you great and mighty things. Sis, I don't want you to make any more excuses, your kids will be alright, your spouse will be okay, your parents will be fine, people may not understand it now, but once they see this new love for yourself, some will be happy for you and some will envy it because they know they cannot use you anymore and you have found your greatest power, and that's "Self-Love." Okay, I know some of you are like what would I do, and what ideas of self-care can I do? Your sister has you covered, Hunny! Below, are a list of self-care ideas you can do and commit to for 21 days that you will love. Be sure to add to this list because the ideas are limitless, so be creative. But most importantly, create a habit so you will always want to do it, and I have tried many of them myself. I love spending quality time with myself because it is so refreshing and renewing. Enjoy your ME time! Thank me later!

Self-Care Ideas:

1. Take yourself out to breakfast, lunch, or dinner. Better yet, why not do all 3?

2. Take yourself on a movie date!

3. Treat yourself to a manicure and pedicure!

4. Breathe!

5. Listen to music that relaxes and soothes the mind, body, and spirit!

6. Take a walk, hike, run, or jog!

7. Do something artsy like draw, paint, or color a picture!

8. Buy yourself flowers!

9. Listen to a positive podcast or sermon!

10. Write daily affirmations to yourself!

11. Read the Bible!

12. Journal!

13. Pamper yourself with a spa day!

14. Smile!

15. Dance like no one is watching!

16. Binge watch your favorite shows or movies!

17. Learn to say NO! (the best self-care of them all, because this one is most people's major downfall)

THE BUTTERFLY EFFECT:

"You alone are enough. You have nothing
to prove to anyone." - Maya Angelou

10.

The Art of Communication

In this chapter, we are going to talk all about communication and the importance of it. The definition of communication is the imparting or exchanging of information, a message, ideas, or emotions. Communication is such a powerful catalyst that keeps the world forever changing because whether it is good communication or bad communication, we still need it to transform, translate, and transmit in our lives and the lives of those around us.

Okay, now sisters, be honest when I ask you this question. On a scale of 1-10, what number are you on the scale when it comes to having good communication with others? Take some time to think about it and let it sink in before answering. I remember a point in time when I was like a 4 or 5 and I would snap, crackle and pop at any given time. But now, I can honestly say I am like a 7.5. I'm not perfect and continuing to grow every day. Prayerfully, by the time this book gets into your hands, I will be an 8 or 9. I will not say a 10 because that is reaching for me, and that would mean that I will have to be a perfect communicator that makes no mistakes. I know as a human I fall short and make mistakes. I need my heavenly Father to help me correct them. No matter where you are on that scale, whether you are a 2 or 10, know there is always room to grow and become a better version of yourself, but it is all up to you.

I remember growing up my great-grandma used to say, "It's not what you say, but it's how you say it." Can anyone attest to that saying as well? I grew up saying that phrase even when I was the one not honoring what that phrase meant. See, my communication issue was, even if the things I said were coming from a great place, I did not have the delivery of the message to go along with it. It was not until recently this year where God dropped in my spirit that "It is what you say and how you say it" I said to myself, *wow that is true* and we have not been taught the correct teaching in that matter. I know this statement is true because the same way you can say something nice to a person in an aggressive tone, you can also say something mean to someone in a nice tone. You see where I am going with this, Sis? So, from this point on, we must take accountability for what we say to people and the tone we are using when we are conversing with others. Whether you are communicating with someone face to face, emailing them, texting, phoning a friend or loved one, or whoever you communicate with, make sure it is done respectfully in a respectable manner.

Communication looks different for majority of the world and not everyone will talk the same, communicate the same, view things the same, respond the same way as others. The translation of a message from one person to the next depends upon our emotions, cultural situations, and even our location. Did you know that communication has three parts to it? The sender, the message, and the recipient. The sender encodes the message in some type of formal way, whether verbal or in writing, and the recipient meditates on the message to get clarity on how to respond. Now, as I examined the three parts of communication, I instantly got a spiritual download from the Holy Spirit in depth. The Holy Spirit showed me that where there is the sender, the message, and the recipient. He said it is the same way in which he speaks to us. God (sender) said when he gives us a word (message) to give to someone (recipient), and we are obedient and do what he said that we are operating in a three-part communication with him. When he showed me that in the spirit, I was like, "Oh my gosh!" It is the same way but on a much deeper, spiritual level. No matter how we slice it or dice it, communication and relationship is one of the two things that have happened since the beginning of time. It is referenced in the book of Genesis in the Holy Bible, where Adam and Eve were in communion with God and with one another because they were husband and wife. I say that to say, those two things will always forever go round and round forever because there will always be a need for communication and a need to be social and in relations with one another whether it is a spouse, family, friend, job child, or even just a random person.

The most important question to this whole thing is how well do you communicate? Do you listen to respond, or do you listen to really grasp what the person is trying to convey to you? Or are you like how I use to be in the past and listen to respond so you can state your facts and justify what and how you feel without even hearing what the other person is trying to say. Let me be the one to say that's not healthy, Sis, because that used to be me. The importance of listening with your mind, body, and spirit and being really in tune with what the person is saying because while listening, you could discover life-changing information that can be missed if you are constantly talking and not hearing. Say for instance, you do not agree with what the person is saying. It is still respectful to hear all parties out and agree to disagree. Having a healthy debate is okay. I think where it goes wrong is when we get mad when people do not agree with us or when people do not do what we want them to do and that's not fair. Knowing that God has created us all different in many ways and one of the many ways is through communication. Sometimes communicating with others can be a bit challenging due to how were raised, the different terminology or slang we may use, what part of the world we are from. Having a respectful, successful, fun, open-minded dialogue is possible to everyone if only we are willing allow everyone to have their own views on things if there can be a common ground of compromise with love and joy still in our hearts. Remember, speaking how you feel without feeling like you are enclosed in a box because one day you will explode, and it may spill over to the wrong person. So, it is a great idea to make sure we are always honest with ourselves because if we are not, we are just lying to ourselves to try to fit into other people's boxes. Speak your mind but let us make sure it is using words that are healthy, respectful, whole, uplifting, and positive. There is just one more thing I want to leave you with, remember to always think before you speak because you might say something that is worth keeping to yourself that could hurt someone's feelings that you may regret because once it comes out, you cannot take it back.

THE BUTTERFLY EFFECT:

"So, in everything, do to others what you would have them do to you." *Matthew 7:12*

11.

Faith It Until You Make It

Now faith is confidence in what we hope for and assurance about what we do not see, as it states in the Holy Bible (*Hebrews 11:1*). Now, let me tell you, me and faith did not get along at some periods of time in my life. See, I was raised in church my great-grandmother and my Aunt Nee always made sure we did not miss Sunday service, Bible study, rehearsals and all. It was a lot, and if I could be honest, I did not use to always like going due to the fact of having to get up so early. As I got older and was going through my own life struggles that quickly went out the window fast. My shortcomings, highs, lows, heartache, and pain taught me to have faith in God. It's when I got to know God for myself, got to see his hand moving upon my life, and built a personal relationship with him is when it became easier and easier to let go and let God. When you let go and let God, you take your hand off the situation and let God handle those places in your life that have some rough patches that need to be smoothed out. When you relinquish your power and yield in faith to God, you will open yourself up to many blessings and rewards for being obedient. When I was a young girl in my teenage years, I use to be a worrier about everything and everyone. I mean, I would have headaches every day, all day. I would be depressed about life challenges and felt so alone in the world. When I would go through trials and tribulations, I either did not do what I knew I was supposed to do, and that was pray and give everything to God. I would still worry and be stressed because of doubt and fear and not trusting the lord. Being that I did not have a personal relationship with my heavenly father and did not believe that God would work out all my problems and issues, but I could tell everyone else that God would make sure they are okay and make a way for them. How foolish was I sitting up in church all those times and did not have a tiny bit of faith. I only knew God and Jesus based on what I was taught or what the pastor preached every Sunday because I never took out some quiet time with God, have some faith to keep me pressing or I did not pick up my Bible at that time to read for myself. A hot mess that was, I am saying to myself now like how can you not have time for God? The alpha and omega, the beginning and the end, my provider, my friend, wonderful counselor, and everlasting God. When I learned faith, I learned power because I know the lord is always by our side advocating for his children (those who obey and accept him), making sure we are covered, protected, and taken care of. Faith is so powerful and strong when exercised with obedience because, in the Bible, it says if we have faith the size of a mustard seed that we can move mountains and do many great things in our lives *Mat-*

thew 17:20. No faith won't be easy, but it will well be worth it because having faith teaches us patience, and it teaches us to let go of our power and learn to lean on to the Father's power so he can breathe in our direction if we trust him. The Lord said, walk by faith and not by sight (*II Corinthians 5:7*). So, when we do so we are not looking at our situation as the final destination because we know that God is our source in every situation and if he brought us to it, he will most definitely get us through it.

In the Bible, there are many stories shared where believers and followers of Christ had to implement their faith in God even if they could not see in the natural how the full picture would come together, but in the spirit, God is always working behind the scenes on a miracle. It was by faith that Jesus performed so many breakthroughs, signs, and wonders to every place his feet trod It was by faith that the universe was formed by God's command ,and he continues to cause everything to stand at attention. The Bible tells us that it is impossible to please God without faith because anyone who comes to him must believe that he exists, and he rewards those who earnestly seek him (*Hebrews 11:6*).

I remember back in 2019, when I went through several tests that caused me to remain faithful in my walk as a believer and follower of Christ. I went through this big shift after going through a bad breakup, and it caused me to be behind on bills. So, long story short, I ended up calling it quits and moving forward with my life. One month later is when everything that seemed to be falling apart in the natural, but in the spiritual realm, it was coming together. I had to remember that faith without works is dead (James 2:26). So, everything that happened, I had to have some action of faith behind it no matter how much stress, hurt, frustration, and guilt I felt for being disobedient to God. In that year, I was on the verge of getting evicted, not having money sometimes to pay my light bill. I did not have money at times for food, gas, or for some necessities I needed. My car payment was backed up four or five months, and I was also driving uber at the time to make some extra cash. While In prayer one day, I told God that I did not know what was going on and that I was stressing because of everything that was going, and after that day, it is like God reassured me that it was all working out for me because I felt so much peace in my spirit from that point on. I did not let anything stress me. I did not care what was going around me I did not let it get in me. I was so happy, I was singing, I was dancing, shouting, giving God the praises because I knew he was going to handle every situation I had. See, the enemy was mad that he lost because he was hoping I would be depressed, stressing, and worrying, but I switched my mindset and he thought I would fold. God gets the glory for all this, not me at all. He is a very present help in the time of trouble. I tell you, and I thank him so much for his grace, mercy, favor, covering, and blessings over my life. When that woman from the company said, "Ma'am, we are calling because we need the money for your car because it is four/five months behind or we will have to come and repossess the car" I was not worried at all, neither did I get mad at her, even though I wanted to snap at this point. But she was doing her job, so

I replied and told her "Ma'am thank you for calling and notifying me of that, but I do not have the money, and I do not know when I will have the money" I also told her, "I put this situation in God's hands and he will figure it out because I cannot." When I tell people that story they think I'm joking, but I am so serious. I really told her that. We must get to a point in our lives where we are literally walking by faith and not by sight. Because I have so much faith that whatever God has blessed me with, the enemy cannot take it away. I want you all to know that having that kind of faith in the Lord helped me get caught up on all my bills and not have to worry or lack anything In my life, and I am so grateful. No matter what season you are in right now know that it is only a test of your faith and strength before you get promoted to your next level in God. Stay faithful, stay prayerful, know that this is not a punishment from God this is a shift from our heavenly father. If you need some motivation on how to keep your eyes towards the hills where your help, God is there waiting to intercede on your behalf. If you need some encouragement and motivation, just take a look back over your life and see all the times you crossed over to the other side. It was not by happenstance. It was the grace and mercy of Jesus Christ that has kept us all these years. If God did it before, know most certainly, he will do it again.

When we have faith, we have hope and when we have hope, we have a sense of peace and tranquility. Know that we do not fight any battles alone because the Lord Jesus is always there. So, if your faith has been low due to intense trials that life brings or shortcomings know that when you surrender is when God gets the glory, and you gain strength and power through the savior. Your faith in God brings the favor of God because during our heavenly Father's training and testing us, he is also being observant over us to make sure he can trust us with certain blessings he has for us. Continue to press. You are almost there, so do not give up.

THE BUTTERFLY EFFECT:

Faith is taking the first step, even when you
do not see the whole staircase.

-Martin Luther King Jr.

12.

P.O.P

(The Power of Prayer)

What is prayer? My definition of prayer is the world's great-est wireless connection to God's ears. Prayer is the most essential thing we must have the consistency to do every single day because we cannot do anything without it. Prayer is something I depend on whether I am having a good day, a bad day, a happy day, or sad day. Prayer changes everything if only we will pray continually and give thanks in all circumstances (*1 Thessalonians 5:17-18*). When we pray, it is not only to ask for material things or the things that we want, but to pray and show God the gratitude, humbleness, loyalty, adoration, love, obedience and thankfulness in our hearts towards him. One thing that I have learned on my spiritual walk is the more consistent we are in prayer and when we are sincere in our hearts, God hears and will answer them. Prayer is essential, especially right now in this time with everything going on in the world. We should never get too busy in our lives where we are trying to put God in our schedule and plans. First off, he is too big of a God to fit in anything when he is the creator of all things. We should be planning our schedules around God and letting him direct our path, and acknowledging him in everything. I remember when I was young coming up, and even in some of my adult life, I never knew why I was drawn to closets and always found such peace and safeness while in them. I would distance myself away from everyone and go in there for some alone time. I never knew that the closet would be my secret place. I go to war in prayer and talk to God. It is the most beautiful thing I have ever experienced because I just love sitting quietly in the presence of God, "The Great I Am." When I became consistent with my prayer life, I am not going to lie, it used to feel like an eternity because I was just sitting there like, "Okay I'm here," and would sit there quietly while so many thoughts were on my mind. So many things were renting unnecessary space in my brain. As I went in my prayer closet every day or when God nudged me to, the more I was surrounded by his presence and glory. I started to more and more feel a sense of security, closeness, love, and a pull from God, causing me not to want to leave his presence. My prayer closet became my bedroom. I have slept in my prayer closet so many nights. It is my therapy session, my chill area, and my sanctuary where I built my altar before God. Knowing God for myself and not from what someone said he was. This was especially important to me - God knowing my heart towards him was something I wanted my Father to know and see. The communication is beautiful.

I said all of this to you today so that you will learn the power in prayer and know prayers can reach heaven and cause demons to flee, set captives free, heals the sick, save the lost and deliver the oppressed. If you feel like prayer is just yet another task, I challenge you to start off praying for 10 minutes in your secret quiet place with God. As you draw to him, he is going to cling to you and 10 minutes is going to turn in to 30 minutes, 30 minutes is going to turn into 1 hour, and it will continue to magnify. As you put your heavenly Father first, before anyone and anything in your life, you will start to see the windows of heaven open unto you. What do you think your reason for not being consistent in your prayer life is? In my opinion, I feel that people do not like to really pray anymore because they do not see results. What we do not understand is that when we pray, we must believe in our father first, have patience and then believe that what we are asking will be answered according to God's appointed time, but we must have the faith behind it to back it up. A lot of the times, we want God to be this magician that pulls tricks out of a hat. No, that is not the way it is. Most of the time, we are praying selfish prayers or wanting God to bless our mess instead of wanting to be in the perfect, holy will of the Lord. I feel in the spirit that the Holy Spirit is wanting to position you to be a giver and not a receiver all the time. The Lord wants us to give him our time, our attention, our obedience, our loyalty, our consistency, our honesty, our love. He wants all of you will you give all of you to him today? God is the all-knowing, Almighty God, and he knows what we need, when we need it, and how much of it we need. We must start being grateful and thanking him for all he has done, thanking him for closing doors that were meant to harm us, praising him that man's rejection was Gods protection, glorifying him because he continues to reveal, remove, and repair people and things in my life and those connected to me. Praying does not require us to talk all the time and ramble. It also requires that we listen, and I do mean listen closely for his still small voice to guide us along our path with him.

My prayer is that you continue to strengthen your prayer life so that the Lord can pour into you like never. He wants to stir up the river of living water flowing inside of you. He wants to do a new thing in you and through you, and he wants to take you higher, deeper and to new dimensions in him. Will you let him, Sister? You have tried it your way, let him take over the driver seat and steer the wheel now. Try it God's way and watch how prayer causes your life to do a 360. I know because I am the living proof that prayer works, and I am a product of my parents, grandparents, family and my village's prayers. Did you know that you are also a product of prayer? We are very blessed because while we were out there in our mess, God had people interceding on our behalf. One of the reasons we are here today is because we had people praying for us.

I would like to say thank you to everyone who has ever prayed for me, for those who will pray for me, and for those who continuously pray for me. I really appreciate and love you all with the love of God. I pray the Lord continues to bless you abundantly, keep you, elevate you, increase you, celebrate you, promote you, favor you, and cover you in Jesus name, Amen.

THE BUTTERFLY EFFECT:

If you believe, you will receive whatever you ask for
in prayer. Matthew 21:22

13.

I Am Free!

(Riding on freedom)

Have any of you ever felt so trapped within yourself to the point you felt suffocated by the weight of your problems, your life, the world, and your spiritual walk all on your shoulders? I will be the first to attest to this. Boy, oh boy, did I feel like I was just in a world where I was existing and not living the life that was intended for me by God? I was not walking or living in freedom, and my identity was nowhere to be found. My main struggle was being the best version of myself I could be in the natural and in the spiritual. To have freedom is the state of not being imprisoned or enslaved by anyone of anything. What do you need to be freed from today?

Being a follower of Christ Is not easy at all because every day we must die to our flesh and try to be more like Jesus and portray his characteristics in the right way and I fought with myself several times about how I should act, how should I speak, how I was supposed to present myself. There was so much pressure I was putting on myself because of things I heard and seen Christians say I should do or be. I knew that if my heavenly Father was who I knew him to be, then he would want me to be free and live a happy, joyful, peaceful, God-fearing life. One day I went and talked to him in prayer and asked him if he created me to be the person I am. For example, I am funny, I love to dance, I love all genres of music, and I love to have fun and act silly, but why do I feel guilty for being me. I then found my answer reading the word one day in *1 Peter 2:16*. It states "Live as free people, but do not use your freedom as a cover-up for evil; live as God's servants." When I read this verse, it literally set me free because I now know that being a follower of Jesus Christ is walking upright, righteous, being meek, walking in forgiveness, love, purity, power, authority, and grace, to name a few. It means not feeling guilty for how God created you and using our freedom to serve the kingdom of God and one another. When we are using our freedom to be nasty, rude, evil, and working with the enemy, then we are not using our freedom in the correct manner. Be who the Lord created you to be, and make no apologies for it at all. If you are doing the work of the lord, saving souls for the kingdom, dying to your flesh daily, being obedient to the Holy Spirit, repenting daily, and continue to follow all the commandments that God spoke about in the word, you will continue to be blessed by him and receive the gift of eternal life. I know for me it is when I begin to be a follower of Jesus Christ is when I really became all the way free. I have found my true identity. This is by far was the best decision I have made in my entire life. I am in love with this gift that keeps on giving.

I want you all to know that if you are a follower of Christ who is on your spiritual walk with him, you may know by now and have seen that our walk is not a piece of cake. It is his love and our faith that we must continue to keep in unison with one another to overcome and elevate to dimensions and new levels in him. Walking by faith and not by sight is a hard, but a much needed benefit as a believer in Christ is that we must have to get over extremely hard times. We need faith in the happy times in our life as well. That is why I love our heavenly Father so much. He is a God of balance, wisdom, compassion, grace, and such unconditional love. Nothing goes unnoticed to him, and whether we are getting rewarded for something good, or chastised for not being obedient, he still allows us to have a lesson as part of our testimony to grow us, not to harm us, which is all done in graceful love. A God that loves us so much that he sent his only begotten son *John 3:16* to come and save the world from sin so that we may be saved so we can have eternal life and become one of his children; be a part of the kingdom. I want you to know that the Lord created you uniquely and different for a reason. Everyone that picks up their cross and walks with him will be different even though we are all on the same path, just in different vehicles. He wants you to be free. You don't have to be confined in a box. You are not a slave to man or this world. You are free because when you accepted Jesus Christ as your personal savior, you became free, matter fact the next time someone tries to put you in a box, let them know your God is too big for you to fit in a box. We are to use our freedom to be ourselves, serve God, and save souls, but not in a way that it will be a disgrace to the kingdom or doing anything that contradicts what the Holy Bible says. I know the pressure of feeling enslaved feeling like a robot, but when I think about the goodness of Jesus and all that he has done for me, how he delivered and set me free, I get happy and emotional at the same time so full of joy. He is such a good father, and I will forever serve him all the days of my life because he has been too good to me not to praise him. Sisters, be free believers in Christ. You don't have to be so politically correct, all uptight and not being real behind the scenes and in the public eye acting like you have it all together as the Pharisees did in the Bible because they were called hypocrites. Be real, be relatable, be free, be balanced, be you because that is what people need right now. You may be the only church that some people ever encounter and the only Bible they may ever read. Be a light in the world. Do not shrink or dim your light to make others shine. You shine too. You are not a slave! So, therefore, you shall not be enslaved but a free servant of the Lord, using your freedom to cause good. There is no feeling like being free, especially when your freedom is being used for a greater cause other than yourself, but rather for the kingdom of God.

THE BUTTERFLY EFFECT:

"It is for freedom that Christ has set us free. Stand firm, then, and do not let yourselves be burdened again, by a yoke of slavery." *Galatians 5:1*

14.

Change Your Words!
Change Your Life!

Words have a way of shaping our life for better or worse depending on what we speak and put out into the atmosphere. I know most of you have heard one of the most famous scriptures from the Bible in *Proverbs 18:21* it states, "The tongue has the power of life and death, and those who love it will eat its fruit." Reading this scripture really ministers to me and one day it made me look at life in a new way to put things into perspective and learn the power of my words so choose positive words.

When I was just a young girl in my teenage years, I would speak negative words towards myself and sometimes to others. I was not sowing seeds of life but of death, because I was unknowingly killing my future, killing my dreams, and killing my ability to do the things that were way beneath all the turmoil I was facing. I was speaking that way because that is how I was feeling, and my faith was not strong at all at that time in my life, so I went with what I knew. Let me just say, that way did not work for me. Having that thought process on the way I use to think, how I use to talk, and the things I use to do kept me in a place where I was limited, confined, and felt trapped. You know the saying, "When you know better, you do better." Well, as I continued on my journey and got closer to God, I learned that words are very powerful, and we have to make sure we are using them to speak life into ourselves. Also, choosing words that build others up has the power to save a life and change a person for the better.

When you know the power of changing your words, you understand the power of changing your life. When you know that you have the power and the authority of your heavenly father within, you will know that you can name and claim anything in Jesus' name having the faith that it will come to pass because you are being backed by the Lord. I have seen speaking negativity to someone make them cry, make them insecure, it made them have low self-esteem, and made them depressed, hurt and lonely. On the other hand, I have seen that speaking positivity to someone brings them assurance, love, happiness, joy, peace, forgiveness, completeness, and so much laughter. Your words can either heal someone or wound someone, so we remember to be mindful of what we say and how we say things when we are conversing with others.

I sense in the spirit that some of you are at the point where you cannot find the place in your heart, mind, and spirit to think positive or even speak positively over your life because anxiety, fear, your past, and depression is trying to do a number on your heart, mind, spirit, and future. Speak over your atmosphere and command those negative thoughts and voices to leave in Jesus' name. Sometimes it is a hard thing to do, especially when it seems as if your life is a spinning whirlwind. I challenge you, Sisters, to manifest and speak what you want even though you cannot see it just yet. Speak affirmative words that start with "I AM" to yourself. I promise you will see a better version of yourself. Do not be afraid because God has given all his children the authority to speak to whatever those things in our lives are that cause frustration, distractions, turmoil, and lack. One way to confuse that enemy that is trying to have you stuck and hid in this season is to turn your mourning, weeping, and sorrow into praise, joy, a shout, and a heart of thanksgiving. You are embarking on a new level in God that is taking you to higher heights and deeper depths, so it is imperative that you open your heart and spirit to receive all that he has for you. We must get to a place where we only want to be in the Lord's will and not our own selfish will.

Sisters, my prayer is that you will start to speak things that are pleasing to what you want to see in your future. God gave you the power to make your day, so how will you show up today? We can hold our own blessings up just by one word that we speak that is not pleasing to the eyes of God. Your tongue has the license to hurt or heal, so be intentional every day about the words that come out of your mouth. I pray that your past will not continue to control you and keep you limited trying to take the dear life out of you. I pray that God will give you a set of new words, and he restore your mind to a place where you are thinking cheerfully about all the great things that are about to manifest in your life. Do you know your open doors are in your words, your breakthrough is in your words, your deliverance is in your words, and your peace is in your words? Open your mouth and stop letting the enemy keep you silent, speak up Queens and know who your God is!

THE BUTTERFLY EFFECT:

"It only takes one word to change a life, choose wisely" - Darshanelle Coleman-Boyer

15.

Ignite Your Fire!

With Power & Authority

There is a fire burning on the inside of you and its yearning for more of God, for more of his anointing, more of his oil, more of his glory, for more of his presence, more of his love, his grace, and more time to spend with him. You may have reached this place in your spiritual walk where you are on fire for God and you are hungry and thirsty for more of what he wants to do in you and through you. God wants to take you to different realms and deeper dimensions in him if you are willing to be obedient to his direction and the narrow path he wants to take you down. Your fire is bringing you power in this hour, so do not put it out, Queen. You have finally reached the place where you are walking boldly in who he has called you to be, even if that means leaving some people behind. You are in the space where people are going to either get with it or get lost, and they have no other choice but to respect your growth as a person and to respect the God in you because

God will most definitely prove himself to others about what he is doing in your life. Your fire is taking you places you have never imagined or even seen before that will surprise you. Your loyalty to Jesus in this season of your life is bringing you much royalty (as my spiritual mom Terri Raven likes to say) for all your hard work and endurance for him. When we spark the fire within us and flow in the Holy Spirit, we are helping someone else to be free, be encouraged, motivated and soar to their next level in God.

Igniting your fire is not easy, and it is not for the weak, because you will have to go through some hard and sometimes dark situations and circumstances to come out on the other side as pure gold untouched with no trace of smoke. When your fire has been ignited, it means you have been filled with the Holy Spirit and bold for Jesus. Being radical for the Lord will have you not caring what anyone says, thinks or feels when they try to come against you because you know God is ahead of everything you are doing. An example of being radical for the Lord will consist of the Holy Spirit having you do things that make you look silly and crazy, but you do not care because you know the Lord has commanded you to do it, so you must obey. When we have this type of fire burning within us, and we activate it through the Holy Spirit, we allow God to work in our lives, and he will take us to places we have never seen spiritually.

One thing that I have learned is when we lose our lives as we have known for so long to follow God is when we find our real lives in which we were created and when we try to save, or lives is when we lose it to the world and other things. God talked about that in the bible in the book of *Matthew 16:25*. Taking up our crosses daily is very imperative on our spiritual walk, denying our flesh and being willing and ready to be used by God at any time he speaks. Continue to walk in your power. You got this, and do not forget to keep your fire burning and your light shining for the world to see because God will use your life to be evidence that he lives, and the blood of Jesus still works.

THE BUTTERFLY EFFECT:

Find your PURPOSE, let it SPARK!!

IGNITE the FIRE within you!!

-Darshanelle Coleman-Boyer

FUN BUTTERFLY FACT:

In the fourth stage, once the butterfly is ready to emerge, the case around the pupa splits open. The wings are wet, soft, and wrinkled against the body, so it cannot take off yet. The butterfly waits for its wings to dry and pumps hemolymph into them so they can become big and strong. Once fit to fly, the butterfly takes off looking for flowers to feed on and other butterflies to mate with. Pretty awesome, right? Who knew?

Stage 4

{ELEVATION TIME! NOW YOU ARE READY!}

Congratulations butterflies! You have finally made it to the end of your forever healing and growth journey. Hence, I said forever, because in life, we will always be faced with things that will cause us to heal and grow. Can I be the first one to tell you that I am ecstatic that you did not give up, but you decided to push past everything that wanted to stop you and count you out and everything that wanted you to quit while on this journey? This last stage will prove if you have really grown up and allowed yourself to heal from those things that were once cages that kept you isolated and bound at the beginning of this journey. All of what you have learned since you have started this book has prepared you for your elevation season. You have been tested, tried and proven by God. So, here is your promotion. I know choosing yourself was not easy, but you put faith in yourself, and you had faith in God to get through. You are now ready to walk in your gifts, talents, your anointing, and your calling, so walk in it with grace, joy, humility, happiness and love. It is by the Lord's grace that he has allowed you to come so far on your journey because many do not make it this far. You have done it, Queens. You are now ready to elevate, overtake, and recover everything you thought you lost. You have overcome all that was designed to make you throw in the tile, but you proved there is no quit in you. You fought the good fight of faith. Now get ready for the increase, the overflow, more than enough, and excess. Stay in expectation of it because it is hitting your life right now.

16.

Your Gifts Will Make
Room for You

All of us were born with a purpose, talents, abilities, and gifts that were given to us by God. I love the fact that our heavenly father strategically had us in mind while he was creating us, and even though everyone in the world will share the same vision, goals, gifts, and calling as someone else, God still made it so that we will remain unique because no one can be you and you cannot be anyone else. Each person has their own special sauce to the recipe, so even though they have seen the recipe before, they have not seen that you have different ingredients, and yours may look the same but taste different from everyone else's they have tasted. That was me speaking metaphorically to get you to see the point in which I am trying to make when knowing and addressing your gifts & talents in your life. I do not care how many people are doing what you have the passion and love to do because if God called you to do it, just know he has made an alleyway for you to do it.

Do not shy away from wanting to do hair, wanting to become a make-up artist, being a real estate agent, being an artist, being a singer, being a motivational speaker, being a teacher, being a life coach, or having a ministry because when I tell you the Lord will favor you and bring you from the back to the front and give you much insight and help you to do it. I hear and see people often and even with myself in the past being a victim of it say, "It's too many people doing that, I don't want to do that!" Not having the wisdom of knowing if God made it a passion of mine, if it is in his will and I am walking into it with great intentions with a pure heart, it will be blessed. Everyone that is in the same area of gifting as you were not anointed by the Lord to do it, and some were flesh led by themselves and in it for the wrong reason. I said all of this to encourage you to go after those dreams and passions that are locked up inside of you. Do not let another day go by and you stay locked up in people prison because you think they are going to say something or think you are trying to be like them, but you let them know that God can give the same vision to more than one person genuinely and use you both in two totally different ways. Now, there are some instances where you have people trying to imitate and emulate other people's gifts, anointing, and abilities, and we must have a watchful eye about that as well. No matter how people try to slice it, dice it, or cut it, there is only one you, and you cannot be replicated.

In *Proverbs 18:16* it states, "A man's gift makes room for him and brings him before great men." I love the Holy Bible because anything you want to know, it has all the answers for you. Just seeing that scripture reassures me that I do not have to try to be anyone else, imitate anyone else, or get out of alignment with what God has given me because there is something he has put on the inside of me that only I have and has activated me to push and look forward towards the light of Jesus. When we flow freely in our anointing, we allow God to position us into a place where he will only get the glory and not man. When we flow in him, we allow his everlasting power to be activated within us. Sisters, I want to let you know it is better when we are ourselves and not trying to be an imitation of someone else's business, ministry, personality, dreams, or anointing. It just will not work.

I am going to leave this with you - know that only what you do for God will last. You ever see people who have all these things going on, but what they are doing is not producing any fruit or any evidence of God's hand in it, and eventually they are on to the next thing and the next thing. Most of the time, when this happens, it is because they are doing things for their own selfish reasons. It's not lasting because they are not doing it unto the Lord but to give themselves the glory. When we give God back everything he has given to us, he will bless it 100 times better than we ever could if only we will be obedient and trust him. One day I was listening to this song by William McDowell called "Withholding Nothing," which is one of my favorite gospel songs. Towards the end of the song, he said something that stuck out to me that I have always remembered. He said, "When we go after the things, we miss God, but when we chase after God the things will come." Every time I hear that song, and it gets to that part, it blesses me so good. My God! It is so true. When we follow the Lords leading for our life, he will make our crooked path straight and take awesome care of us. Staying on the narrow path with the Lord, not looking to the left or the right, will put us before great men because of our obedience to the father. Walk strong and upright in him and watch the reward you get. Blessings to you as you finish out this stage with a BANG. There is great victory ahead of you.

THE BUTTERFLY EFFECT

"Your gifts are not about you, but who you
can be a blessing to along the journey."

17.

A Heart Full of Gratitude

Do you ever have a chance to sit back and think to yourself, "I am so grateful…" Sometimes we can get so caught up with life and our day-to-day task that we do not show God that we are thankful for what we have now. Reading *Philippians 4:11* has taught me that no matter what situation I am in to remain content. It's finding joy, happiness, or peace in whatever situation you are in, yes, even if it is a rocky one. When we can have this level of contentment, it shows our father our hearts and our gratitude to-wards him. Posturing ourselves in gratitude allows the lord to make ways for us that only he can. If our hearts are filled with praise and gratefulness, we are granting plenty and an overflowing abundance to take over our lives.

Thanking God every day when I open my eyes along with prayer is the blueprint to my day and the secret to staying in a great healing space. When the Holy Spirit summons me to pray each morning, I name & claim each thing I am grateful for so he can know the sincerity of my heart and why I say I am grateful and mean it. I do not think we even realize the power behind looking beyond what we can see in the natural with gratitude, so it can manifest itself in the spiritual. It is so easy to complain and forget how blessed we are! Maintain an attitude of gratitude is something we need to take out time to do every day at some moment on purpose. Regularly giving thanks to God not only shows the amazing things he is doing in our lives, but it also gives us a new lens to look at a situation and have a more positive perspective versus our old stinking thinking way. We are renewed and made new in the presence of his joy and peace when our hearts are positioned to having an attitude of gratitude.

So, I have come up with this gratitude challenge. I want you all to do with me. I am going to start it off first by listing 10 things that I am thankful for and encourage you to try it as well. Are you ready?

1. I Am thankful for the gift of life, for God allowing me to be in the land of the living and seeing another day.

2. I Am thankful for the gift of God's love which he says in the word is the greatest gift of all.

3. I Am thankful for time, it is a precious gift that we all have, and we must make sure we are using it in a positive and wise manner.

4. I Am thankful for peace in God which surpasses all under-standing because no matter what may go on around me, there is the peace of the Lord within me.

5. I Am thankful for my entire family. With all that is going on in the world, love and unity amongst family is im-portant.

6. I Am thankful for joy; only which God can give. Joy un-speakable, the world did not give it, and the world cannot take it away.

7. I Am thankful for my husband, my siblings, my village of friends/sisters, my spiritual mother, and everyone that loves and supports me.

8. I Am thankful for grace and mercy because when I was a mess and the Lord gave me grace and still welcomed me as his child. So, I must make sure I am always extending grace to others.

9. I Am thankful for my personal relationship with my Father. I am glad that I know him for myself and no more of what people have told me. An eternal love that never fades away! I am truly BLESSED!

10. I Am thankful for having a place to call home, food in my refrigerator, clothes on my back, and for all my day-to-day necessities that the Lord provides for me and my family. I

am so grateful, and I do not take it for granted at all because somewhere in the world, someone is praying for what we sometimes find ourselves complaining about.

Your turn now! I would like for all of you to write 10 things below that you are grateful for. Dig into the depths of you and look back at all the things God has done for you and brought you through. A heart of thanksgiving and praise is very essential for your release of blessings in this season.

1. _____

_____

2. _____

_____

3. _____

_____

4. _____

_____

5. _____

_____

6. _____

_____

7. _____

_____

8. _____

_____

9. _____

_____

10. _____

_____

THE BUTTERFLY EFFECT:

"The struggle ends when the Gratitude begin" -Neale Donald Walsh

18.

Relationship Over Religion

I remember being a young girl raised in church. I mean, we never would miss a Sunday. Church was all I knew. We would go to Bible study, morning service, sometimes afternoon and evening service, as well. I mean, church was like our second home. We would have choir rehearsals, and we would be on the praise team, even make up dances for the praise team with my cousins. As I got older, going to church on Sundays was embedded in me, even if I did not know what was going on or understanding the sermon, I still went. It was a tradition for my family, but something hit me one day when I was going through things and did not know what to do. That was the most dangerous place to be in because that gave the enemy an avenue to seep in, and he could care less that I was raised in church because he knew my heart was far from God. What got me was the fact I spent all those years in church seeing people praise, worship, judge, shouting, screaming, crying, speaking in tongues, being messy, lying, pastors doing ungodly things, and the list could go on and on. They never preached on the importance of having a personal one on one relationship with God. We were taught some religious traditions that were passed down from generations and generations about not being able to wear pants, not to get tattoos or you are going to hell, your skirts had to be to the floor, if you wore makeup it was wrong, you could not do this, or that because you are going to hell like I mean so many rules that were making the saints feel enslaved and that made the unbelievers run the other way in fear. Doing this has pushed so many people from having a relationship with God because the church was so caught up in religion that they missed the person who needed prayer and was on the verge of a breakdown, especially our generation because some of the elder seasoned christians are still in a religious mindset while the millennials are being bold, radical and free in Christ. I am going to say, now that was not the way God intended for our spiritual walk with him to be like. I want to make it clear that I am not bashing the church. I am just being transparent and speaking on my experiences. I love the church because that is where I have witnessed some of God's greatest miracles and where I could get prayer if I needed it or food if I did not have any. When I would go through certain trials and tribulations when I was growing up, I did know how to pray. I thought if I was going to church, putting some quarters or dollars in the collection plate and looking after the homeless, I was good until reality hit. I had no faith, I lacked a prayer life, and I had no personal relationship with God. This is not to bash any of the pastors or leaders, but this is to bring awareness that the sheep need to know the importance of having those three things during their walk with Christ, so they do not have to walk around unarmed or lost in the spirit.

When I strayed away as a teenager up to some of my adult years, I did not have a mentor or someone by my side to hold me accountable for my actions. I struggled mostly because I did not have my Abba father in my life to guide me or show me the way. It was a while after being on my spiritual walk where I finally let go of religion and started searching and seeking a personal relationship with the Lord. Religion kept me bound in fear, uncertainty. It had me mad. I was lukewarm and kept questioning so much. I wanted to ask God questions, but religion said I could not. I wanted to be me, but being me felt like a caged bird, I wanted to feel alive, free, and have fun, but religion said I had to be serious, always politically correct and perfect. Religion will cause a person to be deeply grieved if they do not know any better.

One day I sat down and talked with God personally and cried out to him, I mean boohoo ugly crying to him. I asked him if he created me to be the person I am, why does religion make me feel like I must be in a box? I told him he created me to be a music lover of most genres. I love to have fun. I love to dance. I love being around family. I love acting silly. I just love enjoying life. I later learned that was not what the Lord desired for his children. He said for us to walk in freedom, but not to use our freedom to do evil (*1 Peter 2:16.*) Surprisingly, I was not the only believer that felt this way. So many other believers felt this way as well, and that made me feel better knowing I was not alone. I am free because my Father in heaven says I am free in *II Corinthians 3:17*. Since I have gained knowledge of what the Lord said, no one, not the enemy, not man, and not even religion can keep me bound anymore. I got away because my Savior came and caught me before I fell in troubled waters. Be who God called you to be and make no apologies for it. This is our time and our new season, so walk into it. Be the light and spread it by doing the works of the lord and pleasing him.

The difference between religion and relationship is religion allows you to be like the Pharisees, where being traditional and hypocritical is normalized. It prevents you from hearing the Holy Spirit and hearing God's voice. It prohibits you from being reachable, relatable and transparent where people can hear your testimony and feel inspired. People who are religious are masked behind the idea of playing church and appear to the world as having it all together just playing the part when behind closed doors they could be the most judgmental people you have ever met. I have seen some very not so pleasant experiences in the religious churches that were totally against what I later found out God was not pleased with. Again, this is not bashing church because I love some good ole fellowship and a great word that will set the roof of the building on fire, okay. My main concern is to get the world's eyes back on our heavenly father and to find him in communion and relationship. Over the centuries and decades, it has been so many lies and cover-up when it comes to the word and our savior Jesus Christ, and that is why the Lord is calling us into deeper relationship with him and knowing him for ourselves, so we do not get easily swayed by delusions and demonic forces in this world. Whereas, a relationship with God, you are going to seek counsel about everything to God in prayer, you are going to have to fast and pray so can last, you will have to be okay with being set apart and being by yourself sometimes, you have to walk in boldness and be obedient to the holy spirit, you will have to sacrifice a lot, having a personal relationship with the father you will have to be tested, tried, and proven through trials, tribulations, and warfare, you will most definitely have to be humble, quiet and graceful, you will have to go through much persecution where you will get lied on, talked about, abused, hurt, etc. the point I am trying to make is there will be some tough times as a servant of the lord, but it's not to harm or punish you, sis believe it or not it is actually helping you to become a better woman and person I can attest to and be living proof of that. Every test is helping you get stronger and stronger in the spirit so you can have more faith and endurance when going through trials as you embark on new levels with different devils. Our walk with Christ prepares us and postures us for greatness if we stick with the blueprint he has given us for our life, and in in the end, he will reward those who diligently seek him (*Hebrews 11:6*).

My sisters, as you all know we are living in some very trying times, and we are living in a Bible story right now. So, it is very imperative that we all really press in and find a personal relationship with God. Things are happening at a rapid rate and people are leaving from here left and right. I want you all to try him and get to know him for you. Not for what mama, daddy, auntie, or uncle said but find him and talk to him for your own good. My prayer is that you will not follow the crowded, busy road of trends that everyone else is following. Abba Father is on the straight and narrow road where not a lot of people are traveling. Choose God today because he loves you and has never failed you, even after all these years. He has never left you. He has promised in his word. God is doing a new thing in you, and in this generation. You just wait and see. You are needed. Keep going and do not give up. He needs you to be bold, to be on fire in the spirit, and he needs you to be prepared. You can do all thing through Christ that strengthens you (*Philippians 4:13*).

THE BUTTERFLY EFFECT:

I am the vine; you are the branches. Whoever abides
in me and I in him, he it is that bears much fruit,
For apart from me you can do nothing John 15:5

19.

Walking Out

Your God-Given Purpose

Do you know there are millions of people walking around every day not knowing their purpose and the reasoning why they were created? Walking in that unknown is scary and a lot of times leads us down pointless and unnecessary roads. Do you know the richest place in the world? If you said the graveyard, you are absolutely correct. There are so many people who leave this life so full of purpose but not discovering it. They died full of unmet dreams, full of ideas, gifts, talents, and abilities. They never went after any of them. If you think about it, it puts things into perspective and makes you think with the mindset of finding your purpose in God and going after your dreams with him. We want to die empty and not full because if we are full, that means we have not and did not do all the things God intended for us to go after our dreams and desires. Although, that can be tricky sometimes because we really must be mindful and understand that not all the times our wants, needs, careers, jobs and our version of our purpose is what our heavenly father sees for us or created us to be. In our natural walk and spiritual walk, we must be intentional about our actions, our thoughts, our words, and how we live our life. Only what we do for the Lord will last. As I stated previously, anything outside of that is just pointless in my opinion. It is a distraction taking us off course. This is why it is important to have the right voices around us like a parent, mentor, life coach, therapist, friend or whoever that will motivate us, hold us accountable, encourage us, pray for us, and support us.

When you are living out your God-given purpose, you are walking into your own destiny that was fearfully, wonderfully, tailored, and created for you. Do not let the paths of others discourage your own progress no matter how long it may take you to get there. Social media is the biggest enemy. We can either use it to our own advantage to promote our businesses, to be positive and help others, or it can have the power over us where it causes us to be distracted, focusing on what other people are doing, and missing the mark of the higher calling of the Lord. Occasionally, I take social media fast when I feel I am getting distracted or utilizing it too much. I take a step back and do a fast when the Holy Spirit unctions me. Sometimes we feel out of place and all over the place because social media is doing a number by keeping us engaged in nonsense instead of focusing on the things that have been on us to do for days, weeks, months, and yes, even years. We have to a daily self-assessment to check in with our emotions, feelings, and moods so we can carry those things within us out in the correct heart and mind. Having the willpower over social media and not letting it have the power over us is what we must strive for often.

See, before we were even thought of by our parents, our Father knew us and had a need of us (*Jeremiah 1:5*). The Lord knew what we were going to be, the things we would have to endure. He knew how our purpose would touch so many lives around the world. I mean, he knows us from inside out, top to bottom. He even knows the number of hairs we have on our head. That's how amazing and detailed he is *Matthew 10:30*. I say to people all of the time that may be struggling with finding their purpose, "Your purpose is wrapped up in your passion." I tell them you will know what your purpose is because it will not leave you alone. I also tell people you will know what your purpose is because you will be able to do it for free and not get paid for it. So, if there is something on your heart and you feel like it is your purpose, examine yourself and ask yourself, *could I do this for free and be happy without getting and money.* Some of you may already be operating in your gift and purpose, not even realizing it. You have been giving it away for free because it is something you do so freely from the heart and soul, even if it is challenging at times. You envision it. You think about it day in and day out. You dream about it, you talk about it a lot, and you live it every day.

Living out your purpose for the lord is walking the right walk, speaking the right tone, and living in such a way where others will see the Jesus in you and living out the life that was given to you by

God. Some of you may be in a place where you do not know what your purpose is, and that is okay now all you have to do is take out time with yourself to dig deep and search yourself to see what drives you, motivate your spirit, and address what your passions are because under that lies your purpose. Spending time with the Lord also, asking him to reveal to you why you were created and all he is wanting you to do in your life and through it. Eventually, it will be revealed to you, and when the time is right, the Holy Spirit will push you out there to pursue it, and no one will be able to hold you back from doing what is ordained by the father. I remember when I was eighteen years old, not knowing my purpose in life, which is the case for most eighteen-year olds. But I was so eager and determined to know. I was on a mission, trying to find out why I was created and wanting to discover my place in this big world. Everyone has an assignment that we must carry out until we leave this earth, and it is our responsibility to find out what that is. You may have to be set apart for a while, you may lose some friends, you may go through a period of feeling alone which you a really not because God is with you, you will grow in a way where you will not recognize your own self in a good way. You will have spiritual CPR and a spiritual heart transplant performed that will have people trying to figure out what is different bout you. But the only difference you can tell people is that you found the Lord. It will be the light of Jesus shining from within you for all the world to see, but it is not about you. It is about spreading the gospel of Jesus Christ and saving souls for the Kingdom. The sky's the limit, and the world is yours as long as you put the Lord our God first in all you do, you will go many places & do great things in this limitless world. Always remember that with man, it is impossible, but with God, all things are possible. Do you know your purpose and why you were created?

THE BUTTERFLY EFFECT:

If you cannot figure out your purpose, figure out your passion. For your passion will lead you right into purpose.   -Bishop T.D Jakes

20.

You Are Now a Graceful Butterfly
(Rise, Soar, Fly)

If you follow steps 1 through 20, you will become a new blossomed individual that is ready to leave your mark in this world. You have been through the valley, the dark days and nights, the ups, downs, highs and lows; you still persevered and was determined to push yourself to the finish line. You have done the self-work, and others will quickly realize there is a light about you that shines from within, a bright light that only the Lord can give. On this journey, I am sure you have lost those who meant you any good, and you have gained those who are meant to go with you to your new level of elevation. Continue to trust every process that the Lord takes you through because he knows best for your life. You were created to shine, to stand out. You were meant to be as beautiful, as powHERful, and stronger than what you may think you are. You have excelled from being a victim to being victorious over every area of your life. Your strength has been displayed for all to see and you have been the living proof that no matter the curves that life throws to you, you can still be clothed in the lord's strength and still stand strong with courage after all. Your testimony that others will be able to see will be "You many have bent, but you didn't break" you have survived what someone else died in, and that is a blessing because God has been with you always. The blessed part about going through trials and tribulations is God gracefully breaks us in the spirit so we can minister to others about what we have endured and how we got over with the Father. Sisters, you are still here for a special purpose and know that God only gives his toughest battles to his strongest soldiers, so know as you continue on in this world with many things that we are faced with daily, know that as long as you keep Abba Father first in everything and you will be okay. This spiritual walk is not easy at all and we cannot do it alone, so we always need Jesus. We do not have to handle this life with our own strength. Just know, you do not have to put so much pressure and stress on yourself, for you are human, and you will make mistakes. God gives us brand new grace and mercy daily to be renewed and restored daily with his heavenly benefits. We are all a continual work in progress, and I am so happy for all of you to start your journey and apply all that you have learned while in this time. I thank you all for allowing me to bring forth the words within this book to all of you. I hope they bring healing, love, insight, unity, and the power of the Holy Spirit. Go out into this world and pass along the gems that were given to you, for that is how we become servants of God, spreading his

word, his light, and his help for others through us. This book ex-
emplifies God's character of being a gift that keeps on giving—
filling us up in the spirit with spiritual meat that we can chew on
for days, weeks, months, and even years to come.

THE BUTTERFLY EFFECT:

You are NOW a Graceful
Butterfly!

21.

A Love Letter from God

Dear My Beloved,

You may think I am upset with you because of the things you have done and the way you have been living, but I am not. Every step you have taken living as your own God and doing the things you wanted to do has led you here to this very moment. I was saddened that you did not know you could come to me and give me all your problems, hurt, pain and trials. I am sad because you chose everything else and everyone else. Even though I have been here all along, I have never left your side, and I never will. There is nothing too bad that you have done that I will not forgive you. I want to invite you back to me; I want to welcome you to me if you do not know me for, I want to show you great and mighty things. Know that my way is the only way, my way is the truth and life. My Beloved, you can rest in me knowing that I have held you in the palm of my hands since you were in your mother's womb. Do you know I know your name, the number of hairs you have on your head, the very depths of your heart and soul? There is nothing you can hide from me ever; I love you forever and ever; my love is unconditional. I want you to be a part of my kingdom, and I need you to follow my lead and where I take you. Just trust me and know that I will never leave you! My Beloved, do you believe that Jesus died on the cross for your sins? Do you believe he rose on the third day and that he is still alive in the spirit? Do you believe he will return, and you will go with him to live eternally? If you have answered yes to all these questions, I want to welcome you, my child. Worship me in spirit and in truth, acknowledge me, draw near to me and I will draw near to you. You are free, so walk freely in me, shining your light everywhere you go. Count your blessings and know my child that you are blessed & highly favored. Bask in my presence, spend time with me, and love on me for that opens my heavenly curtains. Leave your old life and take up your cross to your new life and follow my commands, my teachings, my life, and be obedient to all the things I tell you. You are so strong, for you have given your strength to the wrong people and things. Now it is time to give it to me! I love you, child and I look forward to building an eternal relationship together.

-your heavenly Father

What fears are you letting go of today?

_____

_____

_____

_____

_____

_____

_____

_____

_____

_____

_____

_____

_____

_____

_____

_____

_____

_____

What things that are negatively affecting you are you leaving behind and what new intentions are you setting for your life?

_____

_____

_____

_____

_____

_____

_____

_____

_____

_____

_____

_____

_____

_____

_____

_____

_____

_____

_____

_____

_____

_____

_____

_____

Write affirmations below that start with "I AM" that identify with whom you were created to be and who God says you are? (Ex. I Am Blessed)

If you could write a letter to your younger self, what would it say? What would you tell her? Pour your heart out to her and save her today. How do you feel about writing to her today? Dig deep within and tell her all the things you have always wanted to tell her.

_____

_____

_____

_____

_____

_____

_____

_____

_____

_____

_____

_____

_____

_____

_____

_____

_____

_____

_____

In loving memory,

My Dear sweet Guardian Angel

You were the martriach, the Queen, my strength, my covering, my protection, my heart and a very powerful, Courageous, selfless woman who loved helping others and loved the Lord! We miss & love you so much! Life is not the same without you, but I know the lord needed you more! Keep resting in the arms of the lord and watching over us all. Your legacy will continue on through me. Thank you for setting such a great example of excellence! Your Royalty Reigns forever!

Ola Grace Cunningham

10/31/1939-12/06/2020

Made in the USA
Columbia, SC
26 April 2021